CRIMINAL VIOLENCE: WHAT DIRECTION NOW FOR WAR ON CRIME?

PREPARED BY THE PUBLIC AGENDA FOUNDATION

CONTENTS

EPIDEMIC OF VIOLENCE: NEW FERMENT OVER CRIME AND PUNISHMENT

"At a time when fear of crime pervades American life, there is deep discontent with the criminal justice system and its inability to stem the tide of violence. But no consensus exists about the best way to come to grips with the problem."

Violent crime — rape, robbery, assault, and homicide — is an all-too-familiar feature of American life, a staple item in newspapers and TV news. Day after day, the papers are filled with stories about a teenager who stabs another over a pair of Nikes, or an innocent bystander who is killed by gunfire in a turf battle between drug dealers. No matter where you live in the United States, TV news shows routinely begin with live coverage from the scene of some crime — a brutal rape or an attack on a locally prominent figure who is robbed at gunpoint. The fact that so many of these incidents appear senseless and unpremeditated adds to our fear that they may be repeated, randomly and irrationally, even closer to home.

In 1989, an incident that took place in New York City's Central Park involved such wanton viciousness that it attracted nationwide attention. After spotting a 28-year-old woman on a jogging path in the park, eight youths — none of them under the influence of drugs and all from solid working-class families — attacked and raped her, and made off with nothing more than the sandwich she was carrying. After bashing the woman with a rock and a 12-inch metal pipe, they left her for dead.

Although New York City has long had more than its share of violence, every region of the country has its tales of violent crime. Late in 1991, news accounts in Washington, D.C., featured the case of "Little Man" James, who was arrested for murder. On the night of the murder, James was driving along an inner-city street with friends, one of whom testified that James said he felt like "busting someone." So he took out a gun, shot at a passing car, and killed a 36-year-old woman.

In Houston, where victims of a series of attacks were chosen by the expensive watches they wore, news accounts were filled for months with details about the "Rolex Robberies." Thieves picked out their victims in shopping mall parking lots and followed them home, where armed robberies led to several shootings and at least one murder.

In the suburbs of Boston, a recurring

4

news story features what police call "home invasions." Armed with automatic weapons and machetes, gangs of young Asians invade the homes of prominent Asian businessmen, terrorize them and their families, and rob them of cash and jewelry.

While violent crime has long been a feature of urban life in large cities such as New York, Washington, D.C., Houston, and Boston, according to FBI statistics it is increasing most rapidly in suburban areas and middle-sized cities. Austin, Texas, for example, was traumatized in 1991 by the "Yogurt Murder." During a robbery that took place in a frozen yogurt shop on December 6, 1991, four teenaged girls were shot and burned beyond recognition.

In Charlotte, North Carolina, a mid-sized city that until recently had a fairly low rate of violent crime, residents and city officials worry about the fact that 115 murders took place during 1991, a new record. For the first few months of 1992, Charlotte's homicide rate was higher still. "You wonder who's going to be next and how it's going to tear us apart," says Odell Beasley, an undertaker who buried several of the victims.

Among adolescents, this rash of violence has been particularly evident. Especially in urban America, teenagers often use knives or guns to settle disputes that not long ago were settled with insults and fists. Federal studies show that one high school student in five now carries a weapon — for status or for self-defense — and one in twenty carries a gun.

"Unless violent crime is checked, and checked soon," as former Attorney General Dick Thornburgh said in introductory remarks at a March 1991 "summit meeting" of U.S. law enforcement officials, "we may well jeopardize the first civil right of every American: the right to be free from fear in our homes, on our streets, and in our

VIOLENT CRIME: HIGH AND RISING
Incidents per 100,000 Americans

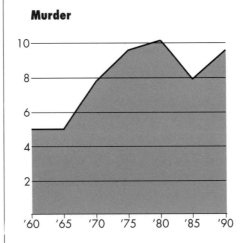

Murder

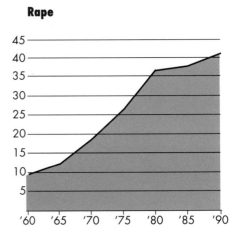

Rape

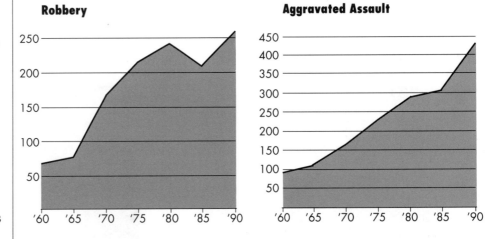

Robbery

Aggravated Assault

Source: U.S. Department of Justice, Federal Bureau of Investigation, Uniform Crime Report

communities. The American people demand action to stop criminal violence, whatever its causes."

VICTIMS OF VIOLENCE

Although the news media often pander to the public's fascination with violent crime and stoke fears unnecessarily, such widely publicized incidents illustrate a disturbing trend.

According to the FBI's Uniform Crime Report, since 1960 the number of violent crimes committed per capita in the United States has increased by more than 450 percent. Recent figures show that violence is still on the rise. The report's statistics for 1990 showed a 10 percent rise over the previous year in overall violent crime. As a March 1991 report from the Senate Judiciary Committee noted, "1990 was the bloodiest year in modern U.S. history, with the murder toll jumping to an all-time record of 23,440." Unfortunately, that record didn't stand for long. Judging by preliminary tallies, over 24,000 murders took place in 1991.

The rate at which violent crime takes place in the United States is a startling and sobering reminder of who we are. The U.S. homicide rate is the highest in the world. In this country, about 10 killings take place per year for every 100,000 people; in vivid contrast, the rate in Britain is 5.5, and in Japan just 1.3.

While killings take place most often in large cities such as Dallas and Washington, D.C., (both of which set new records for homicide in 1991), smaller cities such as San Antonio and Anchorage also registered more homicides than ever before in 1991. It is a sign of the times that the Federal Centers for Disease Control, whose task is to investigate the outbreak of disease, now regard murder as an epidemic.

It is no longer rare to be a victim of violent crime. According to the National Crime Victimization Survey, at least 1 member in about 4.5 million households — which represents 5 percent of the nation's households — was a victim of violent crime in 1990. Twenty percent of all Americans say they have been victimized at least once. Among blacks, who are more often involved in violent crime, as victims and as perpetrators, almost 30 percent have been victimized.

As startling as these statistics are, they tell only part of the story. They do not convey the sense of violation that most Americans feel, or the growing fear. Most Americans are convinced that the crime problem is getting worse. When the Louis Harris firm asked a nationwide sample in 1991 whether they feel that the crime rate in their community has been increasing,

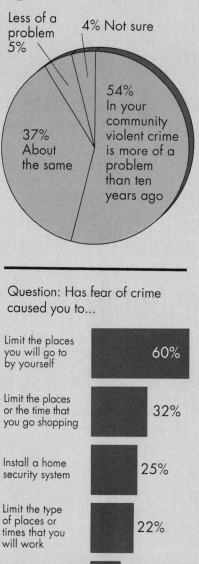

PUBLIC FEARS

Question: In your community (city), do you think that violent crime is more of a problem than it was ten years ago, less of a problem than it was ten years ago, or is it about the same?

Less of a problem 5%

4% Not sure

54% In your community violent crime is more of a problem than ten years ago

37% About the same

Question: Has fear of crime caused you to...

Limit the places you will go to by yourself — 60%

Limit the places or the time that you go shopping — 32%

Install a home security system — 25%

Limit the type of places or times that you will work — 22%

Purchase a weapon for self-protection — 18%

Source: Survey by Schulman Ronca Bucuvalas for the National Victim Center, March 8-17, 1991

decreasing, or whether it has remained the same, 55 percent of the respondents said it is increasing while just 5 percent said it is decreasing.

The fear of violent crime pervades American life, causing subtle and dramatic changes in the way people live. Fearful of being victimized, many people no longer exercise outdoors. They refrain from wearing jewelry and using cash machines after dark. According to a 1991 survey for the National Victim Center, because of fear of crime, 60 percent of the respondents said they limit the places they go by themselves. Taking their safety into their own hands, a quarter of all families have installed home security systems.

The most dramatic indication of a loss of faith in the criminal justice system is that almost one in five Americans has purchased a weapon for self-protection. Gun sales, which doubled in the United States between 1950 and 1970, doubled again between 1970 and 1990, according to the Federal Bureau of Alcohol, Tobacco, and Firearms.

Many people have concluded that the only way to protect themselves against a growing threat is to be prepared to use violence in self-defense. In Houston, where a record 671 murders took place in 1991, Jan Selbst, a travel agent who works in the suburbs, bought a gun in self-defense. "Knowing what they may do to you if you don't protect yourself," she says, "I've decided that I'm going to shoot them so dead they won't get up. I am determined to take charge of my daily life." Sue King, a Houston firearms instructor who offers self-defense classes for women, says that many people no longer feel protected by the police and the justice system. "The criminal justice system has cratered," she says, "and you and I pay the price in lack of personal security."

Judging by recent surveys of the public's confidence in the criminal

"As startling as crime statistics are, they do not convey the sense of violation that most Americans feel, or the growing fear."

justice system, that sentiment is widely shared. A 1991 study conducted for the National Victim Center found that the police get relatively high grades. Two-thirds of the respondents said that the police deserve a rating of good or excellent. Still, of those who have been victimized by crime, only 15 percent say that the crime was reported and an arrest made. Fewer than a third give the prisons high marks for their role in the criminal justice system. Parole boards came in dead last, with only 22 percent saying they ensure that appropriate sentences are applied and enforced.

At a time when violent crime is a worrisome feature of everyday life for many Americans, the public has little confidence in the system intended to deter crime, to deal with criminals, and to protect the public safety.

GET-TOUGH POLICIES

It is especially disturbing that violent crime has increased despite a concerted effort to deter it. Beginning in the mid-1970s and accelerating with the election of Ronald Reagan in 1980, the United States embarked on a program of more severe punishment for individuals convicted of serious crimes. Speaking to the convention of the International Association of Chiefs of Police in 1981, President Reagan reiterated the premise of that experiment, that crime is pervasive in the United States because the justice system is too lenient on criminals. "The war on crime," said Reagan, "will only be won when an attitude of mind and a change of heart take place in America — when certain truths hold again. Truths like: right and wrong matter. Individuals are responsible for their actions. Retribution should be swift and sure for those who prey upon the innocent."

ROB NELSON/BLACK STAR

Learning how to use guns in self-defense at an Atlanta gun shop.

Throughout the 1980s, the nation resorted to tougher measures to combat crime. In response to the perception that judges and prosecutors frequently let criminals off easy while ignoring the public's right to protection, legislators in many states reduced judicial discretion by mandating prison terms for criminals convicted of some crimes, allowing little or no opportunity for parole.

The clearest evidence of America's get-tough campaign on crime is that more prisoners have been put behind bars for longer terms. As a consequence, the size of the nation's prison population doubled during the 1980s and is still growing rapidly. Today, more than a million Americans are held in prisons and jails. Add to that some three million criminals who are under correctional supervision such as probation or parole, and the courts control four million people — a population larger than the city of Chicago.

The immediate concern is where to find room for the swelling prison population. Because the prison population is growing at a rate that requires 250

new cells per day, corrections is the fastest-growing item in many state budgets. Law enforcement officials estimate that $5 billion per year is needed for construction of new facilities — a sum that puts a severe strain on state budgets. In deficit-plagued California, prison officials project that more than 50,000 additional prison beds will be needed by 1995, which will boost state spending by $1 billion a year.

Currently, because prison construction is not keeping up with need, prisons and jails are filled to overflowing, and wardens in many states have hung out "no vacancy" signs. One-half of the nation's largest jails and prisons have been ordered by courts either to expand their capacity or reduce the number of inmates. Bulging prison populations have led to a reassessment of sentencing practices.

While there is a growing sense of alarm about violent crime and widespread discontent with the criminal justice system, no consensus exists about what should be done or what approach would work better. As a recent *New York Times* editorial put it, "There is extraordinary ferment in the justice system. On one side are calls for lock-'em-up justice. On the other are growing concerns about the devastating cost and questionable long-term results of a historic leap in imprisonment."

A lack of consensus about what to do is evident in many discussions about crime and punishment. If you doubt this, attend a city council meeting on the police budget, a legislative debate on criminal laws, or a convention of judges discussing sentencing. Fundamental differences exist about the purpose of incarceration and about what principle — deterrence, retribution, rehabilitation, or prevention of

IT'S A SERIOUS PROBLEM, BUT IS IT GETTING WORSE?

Jack Webb, who starred as Sergeant Joe Friday in "Dragnet," one of the most popular crime shows on television in the 1950s and 1960s, was famous for the words he spoke to witnesses: "Just the facts, ma'am." As important as it is to determine whether the crime problem is becoming more serious, getting the facts straight is harder than it appears.

Q: I get the impression from watching TV and reading the newspapers that violent crime is much worse today than it was a decade or two ago. Is that accurate?

A: Violent crime *is* a serious problem in the United States. But the extent of the problem is exaggerated by the media. By focusing on violent crime, the media offer a seriously distorted view of the likelihood that individuals will be crime victims.

Q: What sources of information about violent crime are more reliable?

A: The two most reliable measures of violent crime, administered by the Department of Justice, are the Uniform Crime Report (UCR) and the National Crime Survey (NCS).

Drawing on crimes reported to local law enforcement agencies across the country, the Uniform Crime Report provides a crime count for the nation as a whole, as well as for specific regions. Its chief limitation is that, since most crimes are *not* reported, the UCR underestimates the number of crimes committed. It is important to note that a rise in reported robberies, assaults, or rapes, may reflect the fact that enforcement agencies are recording a greater percentage of the crimes that take place. It does not necessarily mean that actual incidents of violence increased at that rate.

Since 1973, the National Crime Survey has collected detailed information on the frequency and nature of violent crimes, as well as crimes against property. It is based on interviews with a nationally representative sample, in which people are asked about crimes suffered by themselves and members of their households, whether or not the crimes were reported to the police.

The victim survey is generally acknowledged to be the most reliable measure of the extent of violent crime. However, the survey is limited in several ways: respondents may either forget about a particular crime or choose for personal reasons not to mention it. Instances of domestic violence, for example, are seriously underreported.

Q: Based on information from these sources, can't we conclude that violent crime has gotten significantly worse in recent years?

A: One fact about violent crime is indisputable. The U.S. is much more violent than other major industrial nations. Our murder rate, for instance, is far higher than in Canada, Western Europe, or Japan.

While statistics on other types of violent crimes are less reliable, it is clear that the United States has more rapes, robberies, and assaults per capita than other affluent nations. But this is nothing new. America has long been a peculiarly violent nation.

Depending on the source you consult, you get a different impression of whether violent crime has increased significantly over the past two decades. While the Uniform Crime Report shows a clear increase in violent crime rates over the past 20 years, the NCS suggests that the rate at which robbery or assault take place today is not much different from the rates of the mid-1970s, when the survey was first conducted.

After examining trends from the NCS, sociologist Christopher Jencks concludes that "While America is more violent today than at many times in its past, it is no more violent than it was during most of the 1970s, and there is no reason for thinking that chaos is just around the corner."

Q: Why are so many people convinced that violent crime is much worse today than it used to be?

A: Again, the media play an important role. When crime rates decline, as they did in the early 1980s, the trend attracts little attention. But when crime rates increase, as they did in the late 1980s, it is headline news and considered a harbinger of things to come.

Also, most reports refer to the *number* of crimes committed, rather than the *rate* at which they are committed. Since the U.S. population is growing, we can expect more incidents of criminal violence.

Q: You've been talking about crime rates for the nation as a whole. Aren't some people more likely to be victims of crime than others?

A: Definitely. Your chance of being a victim of violent crime depends on several factors, such as where you live. Compared to residents of large cities, individuals who live in the suburbs and in small towns are less likely to be crime victims. According to the 1990 NCS, the rate of violent crimes per 1,000 people in central cities was 41. In suburban areas the rate was 25, while in rural areas the rate was 23.

With regard to differences between the sexes, men are more likely to be victims of assault, robbery, and murder than women. As for race, nonwhites are far more likely to be victims of violent crime than whites. In 1989, while the homicide rate among whites was 4.9 per 100,000, the corresponding rate among nonwhites was 28.

crimes by locking up criminals most likely to be high-rate offenders — should guide the sentencing decision. Some people advocate stiffer sentences, the denial of parole, or other measures intended to segregate criminals from the law-abiding majority. Others favor increased efforts to reintegrate offenders into the community by providing drug treatment or job training.

CRIME CONTROL ACT

Differing ideas about what to do were clearly apparent in the debate over a comprehensive anti-crime package that was introduced into Congress as the Crime Control Act of 1990 and then taken up again in the 102nd Congress. The package included a variety of measures intended to make the streets safer, to deter crime, to control the sale of guns, and to deal with repeat offenders.

In June 1991, when the Senate began to consider the administration's anti-crime proposal, a vigorous debate on crime began on Capitol Hill. Some senators backed the administration's bill, which called for measures to attack the symptoms of crime by taking a harsher approach to law enforcement and sentencing. In one of its provisions, the President's bill would permit the courts to consider evidence that is illegally obtained as long as law enforcement officials obtain it in good faith. The bill would impose an automatic prison sentence for ex-criminals caught with a gun in their possession. Moreover, it would authorize the death penalty for an additional 38 federal felonies, and speed the execution of condemned prisoners.

"The public is impatient with sociological explanations of crime when the likelihood that they are going to get knocked on the head is rising every year," says Will Marshall, president of the Progressive Policy Institute. "The

'... And what do you see as the major issue in the upcoming election?...'

public wants to see people who act in immoral ways pay the price."

But some members of Congress are convinced that we have relied too much on harsh punishment. The anti-crime package introduced by House Democratic leaders in July 1991 was an attempt to redefine the debate on law and order by focusing more attention on prevention. Among other measures, the bill calls for expanded drug treatment for prisoners. It would also provide more money for police officers to walk their beats, thus staying in closer touch with their communities than officers who ride in patrol cars. "We've spent a decade punishing people for crimes," says Representative Charles E. Schumer of Brooklyn, "and we've totally ignored preventing crimes from occurring."

NEW CONSENSUS ON CRIME

As the 1992 election season started, there was a widely shared sense that fundamental decisions need to be made and a new consensus achieved about criminal justice and what can be done to stem the tide of violent crime. "It is painfully apparent," writes Elliott Currie, a critic of get-tough policies, "that the decade-long conservative experiment in crime control failed to live up to its promises. The disparity between effort and result tells us that something is clearly wrong with the way we have approached the problem of violent crime in America, and few are happy with the results. But there is no consensus about how we might do better.

"There is a pervasive sense," Currie concludes, "that older ways of thinking about crime have lost their usefulness and credibility. But no convincing alternatives have been put forward to take their place. Our policies toward crime and punishment have simply lost a sense of purpose."

We are faced with fundamental questions about the causes of violent crime, about sentencing alternatives, and about the rules that govern what police are permitted to do in obtaining evidence and apprehending criminals. Fundamental questions have also been raised about the purpose and justification of criminal sanctions. Should judges aim first to mete out equal justice, imposing similar sentences for similar crimes? Or should they give priority to preventing further crime by warehousing individuals thought to be dangerous, tailoring sentences to the offender rather than to the offense? Should the rehabilitation of criminals be a major concern? Or is it more realistic and more consistent with our principles of criminal justice to hold up deterrence as the chief goal of sentencing — that is, making the judgment so harsh that it sets a stern example for other would-be criminals?

Overflowing prisons raise basic issues about the usefulness and the necessity of long prison sentences for many crimes. The question is whether sentencing alternatives would protect the community and help to integrate convicted individuals into community life, while bringing down the cost of the criminal justice system.

In discussions about crime and criminal justice, the objective is to see whether we can reach agreement on a coherent and workable anti-crime strategy that reflects the importance most Americans attach to civil liberties as well as the importance of stopping violent crime. In the course of this discussion, we will consider evidence about what has worked and what has *not* worked. Do stiffer prison sentences deter crime? Do job programs and drug treatment help to keep first offenders from becoming repeat offenders? Can those who commit violent crimes be rehabilitated?

With regard to each of these questions, criminologists and law enforcement experts have something to tell us. Fundamentally, however, this is not a debate that will be resolved by expert testimony. The fundamental question is what should be done over the next few years about violent crime. That decision must be informed by a sense of what is right — which is a matter of judgment that requires collective deliberation.

If we are to move beyond a bitter and visceral response that expresses our frustration with violence more than our considered judgment about how to reduce such acts, we will have to engage in coherent discussion about crime, its causes and remedies.

THREE COURSES OF ACTION

No brief discussion can address more than a part of the crime problem. This issue book is not a comprehensive treatment on crime in its various manifestations. Setting aside other types of crime such as white-collar and organized crime, which are different phenomena and may not respond to the same remedies, our focus here is on violent crime.

At the heart of the debate are three different perspectives about why people commit violent crime, whether deterrence works and rehabilitation is realistic, what parts of the criminal justice system need to be improved, and how criminals should be sentenced.

From the perspective of our first choice, the underlying problem is that American society is too lenient with those who break the laws, thereby encouraging lawlessness. Accordingly, the most promising solution is to get tougher with *all* criminals, to step up enforcement efforts, appoint tougher justices, impose longer jail and prison sentences, and build more prisons.

Advocates of a second choice place their emphasis on dealing with the causes of crime rather than treating the symptoms. From this perspective, unless we recognize the corrosive social and economic forces that lead to criminality and take serious measures to address the causes of crime, we are unlikely to lower the rate of violent crime. While agreeing that dangerous criminals must be locked up, advocates of this view emphasize that alternatives to incarceration must be expanded to deal with the causes of criminal behavior, such as drug addiction and a lack of skills needed for gainful employment.

From the perspective of our third choice, efforts to deal with violent crime must begin by identifying the relatively small group of high-rate offenders, and acknowledging that they are unlikely to be rehabilitated or deterred by the threat of harsh prison sentences. The only realistic way to deal with high-rate criminals is to recognize that they are incorrigible. Considering the threat they pose to society, they must be locked up indefinitely.

Each of these perspectives begins with a distinctive explanation of why people commit crimes. No prescription for the nation's criminal justice system is likely to be effective if it is based on an inaccurate diagnosis. If the diagnosis is wrong, we end up at best treating symptoms, not causes. So this is where the discussion begins, with an exchange of views about why people commit crimes.

But it is important that public debate about violent crime not end there. This is chiefly a discussion about what should be done to combat violent crime. If we are to build a society that is less dangerous, less fearful, less torn by violence, what should be done? That is the topic of these Forums. ∎

CHOICE #1
DETERRENT STRATEGY: GETTING TOUGHER ON CRIMINALS

"Serious crime is committed more frequently today because many people believe they can get away with it, or get off easy. The most promising solution is to get tougher with all criminals, to make it clear that violent acts will not be tolerated."

When the Justice Department announced that violent crime increased in 1990 by 10 percent over the previous year, Dan Eramian, a spokesman for the Attorney General, said the figures were "further evidence of the need to pass a crime bill that is tough on criminals."

That was the theme of comments by administration spokesmen in defense of a new anti-crime bill sent by the White House to Congress in May 1991. Speaking in Washington to an audience of uniformed police and the families of slain officers, President Bush said the measures contained in the proposal would help to stop crime. As the president put it, the proposal aims to "take back the streets by taking criminals off the streets."

Ticking off the bill's main provisions, the president proposed to expand federal prisons to provide space for an additional 24,000 inmates at a cost of $1 billion. If passed into law, he said, the bill would permit hiring 1,600 new federal prosecutors to speed up the judicial process. Moreover, the bill would impose stricter penalties for many crimes. It would expand the number of federal crimes punishable by the death penalty and impose mandatory sentences on repeat felons who use guns.

In another provision, the bill proposed to lift certain restrictions on the kinds of evidence that can be considered in criminal trials, in order to prosecute more criminals. "For too long," the president said, "the scales of justice have been tipped in favor of criminals instead of law-abiding Americans."

The underlying theme of the administration's proposal was that by upping the ante on crime, significant progress could be made in deterring would-be criminals. In the words of White House aide Roger Porter, who helped to write the bill, "The people who are committing these crimes are not dumb. They know what the chances are of getting caught and getting sent to prison. As we increase those odds, we can change their behavior."

DAVID GOTHARD

This approach to crime is based on a diagnosis of the problem that to many people is both obvious and compelling. Serious crime is committed more frequently today because many people figure they can get away with it. Crime has become worse, from this perspective, because American culture has become more permissive and the criminal justice system more lenient. Because the courts and the prison system are overburdened, many criminals who deserve stiff sentences get off easy.

This sentiment is widely shared. Surveys conducted over the past few years by the National Opinion Research Center have found that eight in ten Americans are convinced that the courts do not deal harshly enough with criminals. As a result, justice suffers.

At a time when violent offenders are often able to get away with serious crimes, advocates of this view are convinced that our first priority must be to bolster the system so that criminals are apprehended and given punishment that is swift, certain, and appropriately severe. Unpleasant sanctions teach a useful lesson. They underline the importance of law-abiding behavior, and they deter other would-be criminals. Especially for serious offenders, prison terms — in many cases, long prison terms — are necessary, to teach a lesson both to convicted criminals and would-be criminals. In brief, this perspective on crime and criminal justice rests on the twin pillars of deterrence and retribution.

CALCULATING CRIMINALS

Criminals, from this perspective, are much the same as other people. Like the rest of us, their behavior is governed by the expectation of risks and rewards. In this sense, choosing to commit crime is like choosing a line of work. A substantial number of people examine the

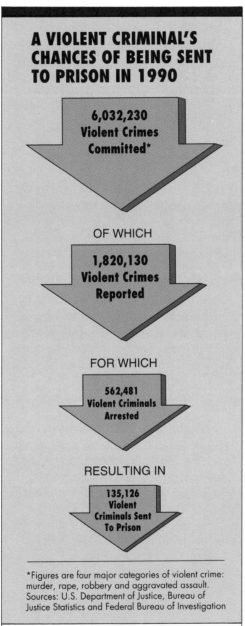

A VIOLENT CRIMINAL'S CHANCES OF BEING SENT TO PRISON IN 1990

6,032,230 Violent Crimes Committed*

OF WHICH

1,820,130 Violent Crimes Reported

FOR WHICH

562,481 Violent Criminals Arrested

RESULTING IN

135,126 Violent Criminals Sent To Prison

*Figures are four major categories of violent crime: murder, rape, robbery and aggravated assault. Sources: U.S. Department of Justice, Bureau of Justice Statistics and Federal Bureau of Investigation

world around them and conclude that crime is a better bet than a "straight" career. To recall Roger Porter's words, people who commit crime "know what the chances are of getting caught and getting sent to prison," and adjust their behavior accordingly.

Most law-abiding citizens — whose view of the justice system is colored by television portrayals of intrepid detectives who generally discover who committed the crime, and courtroom dramas in which juries reach a verdict and justice is done — overestimate both the chances of getting caught and the severity of sentences. But most criminals have more accurate sources of information about the likelihood of apprehension.

As political scientist James Q. Wilson points out, most criminals depend on the accounts of others who have recently had "a run-in with the police and the courts and who, therefore, can supply to their colleagues a crudely accurate rule of thumb. The 'heat is on' or 'the heat is off.' Judge Bruce MacDonald is either 'Maximum Mac' or 'Turn 'em Loose Bruce.'"

Though advocates of this view acknowledge that some crime is impulsive, they believe that most criminal acts involve an element of calculation, as perpetrators weigh benefits against anticipated costs. This applies even to kids involved in crime. Several years ago, anthropologist Sally Engle Merry talked to youthful offenders in an urban neighborhood and observed them over a period of months. She found that even inexperienced offenders operate according to rules of thumb about risks they are likely to encounter. Like most criminals, the youngsters she studied wanted something — money, power, attention, respect — and regarded criminal activity as a direct way of getting it. In choosing their targets, they calculated the odds. They spoke knowledgeably about the likelihood of getting caught in one part of the district rather than another. They talked about which kinds of citizens are most likely to report a crime to the police, and which offenses are most likely to lead to arrest and prosecution. They also talked about what kinds of stories would be believed by judges and juries, in case they are apprehended. While some of

"Accountability under the rule of law is our only real assurance of public safety."

— Dick Thornburgh

their crimes seemed to result from spur-of-the-moment decisions, these youngsters were not indifferent to the consequences.

To advocates of this first perspective on criminal justice, since criminals are calculators, everything possible should be done to ensure that they are apprehended, that justice is swift, and punishment certain. In the words of Dick Thornburgh, speaking to a group of law enforcement officials in March 1991, "Accountability under the rule of law is our only real assurance of public safety."

GETTING AWAY WITH IT

In this light, the fact that 91 percent of all violent crimes do not result in arrest is a fatal flaw in the system and an inducement to criminal activity. The most important thing to notice about the criminal justice system, from this perspective, is how seriously flawed it is at every stage from apprehension to sentencing.

At the first step, people often do get away with serious crimes. A Rand Corporation study shows that the chance of being arrested for any given robbery is only about one in ten. Even those who engage in armed robbery, a more serious felony, manage to escape apprehension seven out of eight times. There are various reasons why the chances of being caught for a particular crime are so low, among them the fact that more than two-thirds of all major crimes are never reported to the police.

Even when suspects are arrested, they often go free. In roughly half of all arrests, charges are dismissed. In some cases, problems result from a failure to find sufficient evidence linking the defendant to the offense. In other cases, problems arise when witnesses fail to appear or when they give inconsistent testimony. When a

prior relationship exists between the victim and the defendant, it is not uncommon for witnesses to decide not to testify.

Finally, as proponents of this view point out, cases are often dismissed because of due process problems. Both police and prosecutors drop cases based on improperly seized evidence. Many advocates of this view are convinced that legal technicalities often take precedence over justice. In the words of Attorney General William Barr, speaking in defense of the administration's proposal to permit evidence in criminal trials seized without search warrants but in good faith, "The system is riddled with loopholes and technicalities that render punishment neither swift nor certain."

In theory, the criminal trial is at the heart of the law enforcement system. In fact, only a small minority of the individuals who are arrested and charged with serious crimes are sub-

jected to trial by jury. This, too, is a concern to those who feel that the justice system offers no sufficient deterrent to criminals.

What actually happens in many cases is that judges and prosecutors rely on plea bargaining. Under this arrangement, the defendant pleads guilty to a lesser charge than is warranted by the facts. Plea bargaining is justified on two grounds. It saves the time and money involved in arranging a trial. Since it results in shorter sentences than those prescribed for the crime committed, plea bargaining helps to ease pressure on overcrowded prisons.

Resorting to plea bargaining may be expedient in the short-run, as advocates of more effective deterrents acknowledge. But they insist that it is unjust for pleas to be "copped" to relatively trivial offenses, especially when

13

DELICATE BALANCE: INDIVIDUAL RIGHTS VS. SOCIETY'S RIGHT TO PROTECTION

Just before he was confirmed as Attorney General in 1991, William P. Barr expressed his frustration with procedural restraints in the justice system in an editorial that appeared in the *New York Times*. "The system," said Barr, "is riddled with loopholes and technicalities that render punishment neither swift nor certain." Barr's comment — and the efforts of some members of Congress to restrict criminal appeals and to give police more freedom as they seek evidence of criminal wrongdoing — represent the latest volleys in a long dispute over procedural rules that apply to the criminal justice system.

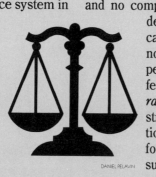
DANIEL PELAVIN

The debate over these rules illustrates the difficulty of achieving a balance between two objectives: protecting individual rights and protecting society by enforcing the laws.

At issue is the interpretation of the Constitution — particularly the Fourth and Fifth Amendments. By guaranteeing due process of law, these Amendments protect individual rights against arbitrary state power.

In recent years, the debate over procedural rules has focused on three issues: what police are permitted to do in extracting confessions from suspects; what police are permitted to do in carrying out searches; and what rights criminals have to appeal their convictions.

SELF-INCRIMINATION

The Fifth Amendment applies at the time of arrest. It protects suspects from being forced to say something that might be self-incriminating. In 1966, in the case of *Miranda* v. *Arizona*, the Supreme Court ruled that, prior to questioning, police must inform suspects of their right to remain silent and to have an attorney.

In many cases, police may suspect that a particular individual committed a crime, but no one witnessed the crime and no compelling circumstantial evidence is available. In such cases, if the suspect chooses not to confess, police are not permitted to extract a confession. As critics of the *Miranda* ruling see it, this restriction on police interrogation of suspects deprives enforcement officials of the suspect's help in solving the crime.

Civil libertarians regard the *Miranda* warning as a modest safeguard against police coercion. Due process begins with the insistence that individuals are innocent until proven guilty. Safeguards of this sort are a way of protecting innocent people against police coercion that may lead to false but self-incriminating statements.

LIMITS ON POLICE SEARCHES

The Fourth Amendment spells out Americans' right to be "secure in their persons, houses, papers, and effects, against unreasonable searches and seizures." As a general rule, in the United States, police are not allowed to enter and search a home without a warrant signed by a judicial officer and issued on "probable cause" that evidence of criminal wrongdoing can be found there. Evidence gained through unauthorized searches cannot be used in court.

To many people, the exclusionary rule symbolizes what has gone wrong with a criminal justice system that seems to care more about individual rights and legal niceties than about bringing criminals to justice. To give the police more latitude, the Bush administration favors changing the laws to permit evidence obtained in warrantless searches conducted in "good faith" to be introduced in criminal trials.

Others oppose such measures on the grounds that they invite abuses of police powers. As civil libertarians see it, weakening the exclusionary rule would encourage abuses of justice while doing little to get dangerous criminals off the street. In support of this claim, the federal government's General Accounting Office notes in a recent report that the exclusionary rule is the reason for throwing out evidence in less than 2 percent of all cases.

THE RIGHT TO APPEAL

Article III of the Constitution ensures that no innocent person will be wrongfully detained. It guarantees anyone convicted of a crime the right to appeal. Some people feel, however, that *habeas corpus* is frequently abused. Because defendants are permitted to pursue an almost endless series of appeals to their cases, the judgment of the criminal justice system is repeatedly called into question.

For deterrence to be effective as a crime-fighting strategy, say those who would limit *habeas corpus*, punishment must be swift and certain.

Accordingly, many people favor restricting prisoners' right to appeal convictions. One version of the anti-crime bill under consideration in the House would bar successive *habeas corpus* petitions unless new facts emerge that could not have been included in a prior petition.

Civil libertarians hold a decidedly different view of the right to challenge a conviction. The absence of finality in sentencing, as they see it, is not a flaw but a virtue of the American judicial system since it recognizes human fallibility. In the words of Samuel Walker, "Protection of individual rights requires recognition of the possibility of error in the criminal justice process."

> "Eight in ten Americans are convinced that the courts do not deal harshly enough with criminals. As a result, justice suffers."

it is almost certain that people who do so are guilty of more serious crimes. For the accused, writes legal scholar Richard E. Morgan, "the plea-bargaining process becomes a sordid crapshoot (albeit with the dice loaded in his favor) rather than a solemn accounting before the community of his guilt or innocence." If we wanted to tell would-be criminals that the court system is prepared to wink at wrongdoers and bargain over their punishment, we could hardly do better than the plea-bargaining process.

At the stage of sentencing, no firm connection exists between the seriousness of the crime and the severity of the sentence. In fact, only about 25 percent of those convicted of violent offenses are sent to prison. The rest are released on probation. Often, it is the number of cells available, not the seriousness of the crime, that determines which defendants will serve what amounts of time.

Even when longer prison terms are specified, they are rarely served. A 1988 report from the Justice Department found that the average murderer spends just six and one-half years behind bars. As prisons become increasingly overcrowded, the average

prison term per robbery has declined — from 57 months in 1986 to 38 months in 1988. "We are incarcerating more people," observes criminologist Lyle Shannon, "but most get out before very long."

Reports of juveniles engaged in criminal activity suggest that they are vividly aware that the penalty for illegal activities — even for violent crime — is often light. In Austin, Texas, older gang members call the younger members "minutemen" because they're likely to be in jail only briefly, then released.

Morgan O. Reynolds, an economist at Texas A&M University, who recently completed a study of serious crime and punishment over the past four decades, says the main reason for the nation's high crime rate is that the likelihood of serious punishment is

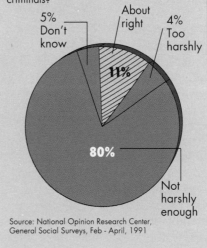

PUNISHING CRIMINALS
Most Americans feel that the courts are too lenient.

■ In general, do you think the courts deal too harshly or not harshly enough with criminals?

5% Don't know

About right

4% Too harshly

11%

80%

Not harshly enough

Source: National Opinion Research Center, General Social Surveys, Feb - April, 1991

lower than it used to be. Consequently, criminals conclude that crime pays. Reynolds' study, conducted at the Dallas-based National Center for Policy Analysis, shows that despite the surge in imprisonment in recent years, the probability of doing time for criminal activity today is less than half what it was during the 1950s.

Overall, as advocates of stiffer deterrents see it, the American criminal justice system is deeply flawed. Its message to would-be criminals is that even if you are caught for a serious crime, you can probably get away rather easily. "Many people," writes James Q. Wilson, who are "watchful, dissembling, and calculating of their chances, ponder our reaction to wickedness as a clue to what they might profitably do. Our actions speak louder than our words. When we profess to believe in deterrence and to value justice, but refuse to spend the energy and money required to produce either, we are sending a clear signal that we think safe streets can be had on the cheap. We thereby trifle with the wicked, make sport of the innocent, and encourage the calculators. Justice suffers, and so do we all."

WHAT SHOULD BE DONE

To proponents of this view of the crime problem, it is clear what should be done. A higher percentage of criminals must be apprehended and given punishments that reflect the seriousness of the crimes they com-

LEGAL TECHNICALITIES

PROSECUTION

DEFENDANT

ASAY/COLORADO SPRINGS GAZETTE TELEGRAPH

mit. Immediate steps must be taken to increase the certainty that those who commit serious crimes are apprehended, found guilty, and punished severely enough to deter other would-be criminals.

It is not in anyone's interest to let criminals off easy, even on their first offense. But as things stand, because of overcrowding, many offenders — particularly juvenile offenders — are arrested and convicted several times before they serve a prison sentence. It is essential, from this perspective, that first offenders be impressed with the seriousness of what they have done. Accordingly, says federal Judge Frank Easterbrook, criminals should be punished the first time they're caught, not let off with a warning and a reprimand. In his words: "If you raise the price of rutabagas, people will buy fewer rutabagas."

As a second step, criminal court procedures should be changed to close legal loopholes such as plea bargaining, the insanity defense, and the exclusionary rule. If such loopholes were closed, punishment would be more certain — and as a result more people would be deterred from crime.

Most of all, say advocates of this perspective, sentencing should be stricter and mandatory sentences should be imposed for many serious crimes. For years, judges were given considerable discretion in sentencing, and sentences tended to be neither fair nor consistent. Under indeterminate sentencing, a defendant might receive a 1 to 25-year sentence, with the understanding that a parole board could decide when the defendant is sufficiently rehabilitated to be released.

Advocates of stringent deterrents to crime oppose indeterminate sentencing and reject the principle of rehabilitation on which such sentences are based. Since the main principles guid-

ing sentencing should be deterrence and retribution rather than rehabilitation, the public is better served by mandatory sentences — fixed sentences for specific crimes, imposed automatically.

Since the 1970s, sentencing laws have been changed in many states, and mandatory sentences are now far more common. In New York State, sentencing procedures put into effect in the 1970s require prison terms for individuals convicted of violent felonies and for those convicted of a second felony.

The premise of mandatory guidelines is that sentencing should not vary from one judge to another. Justice is carried out when all criminals who commit similar crimes receive similar sentences. In its pending crime bill, Congress is considering a proposal to extend mandatory minimums for various crimes.

In 1984, the Federation of New York Judges declared that American society is threatened by "robbers, rapists, and felons of every kind" and recommended an ambitious program of prison construction, because "swift and severe punishment is the only defense against predators." Since then,

the capacity of America's prison system has expanded." As advocates of this choice see it, it is necessary to expand penal institutions still further, for the same reason.

Over the past decade, the United States has made a large investment in prisons. An estimated $30 billion has been spent in construction, to double the system's capacity. This has led to what proponents of this position regard as a notable payoff: Americans are safer because more violent criminals are locked up.

Eugene Methvin, a reporter who has covered the criminal justice system for 40 years, points out that the experience of two states — California and Texas — teaches an important lesson. In California, almost $4 billion has been spent since 1982 to expand the prison system. Throughout the 1980s, the state's inmate population quadrupled. By 1990, says Methvin, "murder, rape, and burglary rates fell by a whopping 24 to 37 percent from their peaks in 1980 to 1982 — which translates as an annual reduction of nearly a thousand murders, 16,000 robberies, and a quarter of a million burglaries."

> "Punishment teaches a moral lesson, not just to the convicted individual but to everyone else. It is a reminder that brutal acts will not be tolerated."

In contrast, says Methvin, the state of Texas skimped on prisons during the same period and paid a high price for doing so. In an effort to curb soaring costs for penal institutions, the Texas state legislature in 1983 adopted a policy of turning prisoners loose faster. The result, as Methvin points out, was that "the crime rate in Texas soared 29 percent between 1980 to 1989, making Texas the second most crime-prone state." The lesson, concludes Methvin, is clear: "Lock 'em up and you slow 'em down. Turn 'em loose and you pay an awful price."

Advocates of this choice concede that imprisonment is an expensive sentencing option. But if multibillion dollar expenditures are necessary to contain violent individuals, to deter would-be criminals, and to protect the public, this is a justifiable expense. "This country ought to adopt a single principle for crime," says Congressman Newt Gingrich. "We should build enough prisons so that every violent criminal in America is locked up, serves real time, and serves out their full sentence. It is possible for a civilized society to find a method to build enough prisons, at a common-sense cost. If that means taking three or four large military bases and allowing the states to build a zone where prisoners are sent, then we ought to do it. If people are determined to be barbarians, we are determined to protect ourselves."

It is time to stop making excuses for those who commit crime, conclude proponents of a get-tough policy, and it is time to stop apologizing for imposing harsh sentences on the individuals who commit those crimes.

Since the early 1980s, the nation's prison capacity has been significantly expanded. In New York State, which has been among the leaders in new prison construction (along with California and Florida), 29 new prisons were built between 1983 and 1991 at a cost of more than $2 billion. Over that period, the number of inmates in New York State prisons increased from about 30,000 to almost 60,000.

Proponents of our first choice are convinced that the United States must continue this hard-nosed policy. In a 1990 study, Morgan Reynolds commented that while the U.S. crime rate is still depressingly high, the rate at which it is rising is slower than it was a few years ago. He attributes this to get-tough attitudes and an increased willingness to impose serious prison sentences. "We have an unpleasant method of crime control — prison — that works," he says, "and some pleasant nostrums that don't work. So we must use the unpleasant methods."

Finally, say advocates of the deterrence strategy, society has a right and an obligation to imprison individuals who resort to criminal violence. Prison sentences reflect society's conviction that criminals should get what they deserve — in a word, retribution.

JUSTICE
SWIFT AND SURE

Punishment also teaches a moral lesson, not just to the convicted individual but to everyone else. It is a reminder that rules are fundamentally important and that brutal acts which threaten the fabric of society will not be tolerated.

In the words of Justice Sandra Day O'Connor: "Our best defense against crime is developing in each generation a sense of right and wrong. The law has a part to play in this process. When society outlaws certain behavior and punishes it with certainty, it establishes a moral tone. In this way, criminal law is an embodiment of society's values, an important way in which society instructs citizens on proper behavior."

WHAT CRITICS SAY

Both as a diagnosis of why people commit serious crime and as a prescription for what should be done, critics reject the get-tough strategy. In the words of columnist Tom Wicker, "The nation's serious crime problem has caused a frightened public and political overreaction — lock up more people for longer periods — that's costing taxpayers dearly, while doing little, if anything, to provide a safer society."

This is the wrong approach, say critics, for several reasons:
- It gives a misleadingly bleak view of the ability of the criminal justice system to apprehend, convict, and apply serious prison sentences for the most dangerous offenders.
- At the same time, it overestimates what the criminal justice system can realistically accomplish in apprehending violent criminals.
- It is based on the mistaken assumption that most individuals who commit serious crimes are "calculators" who will be deterred by the prospect of swifter, more certain, and more severe punishment.
- It prescribes harsh measures that

UNSEEMLY DISTINCTION: WORLD LEADER IN INCARCERATION

Critics are concerned about what they regard as the folly of an anti-crime policy that relies heavily on a lock-'em-up strategy. Frightened by escalating violence, American society has resorted to incarceration as an all-purpose solution. "Today," writes U.S. Appeals Court Judge David L. Bazelon, "devices once justified as means of maintaining order while we examine the roots of crime are dressed up and presented as panaceas."

Over the past decade, the federal prison population more than doubled. Figures from the Bureau of Justice Statistics show that more than one million Americans are now in jail or prison, either serving time or awaiting trial. In 1990, the cost of keeping them in prison and jail was $16 billion.

According to the Sentencing Project, a Washington-based group that promotes new approaches to sentencing, the United States has achieved an unseemly distinction: We imprison a larger share of our population than any other nation. Throughout most of the world, incarceration rates range from about 20 to 140 per 100,000 residents. South Africa, which has the world's second

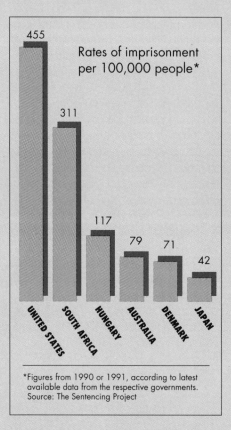

Rates of imprisonment per 100,000 people*

455 — UNITED STATES
311 — SOUTH AFRICA
117 — HUNGARY
79 — AUSTRALIA
71 — DENMARK
42 — JAPAN

*Figures from 1990 or 1991, according to latest available data from the respective governments.
Source: The Sentencing Project

highest imprisonment rate, incarcerates 311 people per 100,000. The United States tops the charts with an overall

incarceration rate of 455 out of every 100,000 residents. Among black men, the rate is a startling 3,370 per 100,000.

At a time when the United States is already the world leader in incarceration, growth in the prison population is pushing the U.S. numbers still higher. If the criminal justice system keeps throwing people into jail and prison during the 1990s at the rate achieved in the 1980s, critics point out that the nation will need 250 new cells per day, which will require an additional $5 billion per year for construction costs alone. Spending on prisons, which in recent years has risen much faster than spending on education, is now one of the largest items in most state budgets. In 1991, state expenditures for corrections rose by 16 percent — the biggest increase in any item on state budgets.

In the words of Daniel O'Brien, assistant Minnesota corrections commissioner, "There's no relationship between the incarceration rate and violent crime. We're in the business of tricking people into thinking that spending hundreds of millions of dollars on new prisons will make them safer."

are counterproductive, such as mandatory sentences and long prison terms.

• It does nothing to address the long-term causes of the crime problem.

For each of these reasons, say critics, devoting even larger sums to build more prisons will do little to make American society safer or to reduce the crime rate.

Regarding the first of these points, critics feel that this approach is based on an inaccurate diagnosis of the problem. America's criminal justice system is not so porous as proponents of a get-

tough strategy suggest. When cases are dismissed, they often involve less serious crimes, especially crimes in which the victim knew the offender or cases in which the evidence is shaky. But, as criminologist Samuel Walker points out, "When a serious crime is committed by a stranger and the evidence is reasonably solid, the system does an effective job of convicting and punishing. For the crimes that count the most, the system is fairly strong. We punish rather severely those major

offenders whom we succeed in catching."

No matter how many resources are poured into it, say critics, the criminal justice system alone cannot prevent most crime and it is unrealistic to expect it to do so. We should acknowledge that the police have a limited ability to control crime. Generally, they can do something about a crime only when it has already occurred and when it has been reported. Even then, the chances of apprehending individuals who commit most street crimes are quite low. Over the past 30 years, as

> "Devoting even larger sums to build more prisons will do little to make American society safer or to reduce the crime rate."

critics of this approach point out, there has never been a time when, for every 100 reported crimes, more than 6 percent of the cases resulted in prison sentences.

Even if far more resources were devoted to enforcement efforts and incarceration, it is unlikely that the chances of a criminal facing imprisonment for a particular crime would be greater than about 10 percent. In other words, say critics, "swift and certain punishment" for the majority of crimes is a mirage. Bolstering enforcement efforts and enlarging prisons are not likely to deter many would-be criminals.

A high rate of incarceration might be justified, critics concede, if it could be shown that it has a unique deterrent effect and that it protects the public by discouraging criminal acts. But as critics see it, attempts to win the war on crime by deterring would-be criminals are bound to fail for a fundamental reason: most criminals are not "calculators" who are likely to be deterred by changing the odds that they will be caught and punished with long prison terms.

The individuals who are most prone to serious crime are what economists call heavy discounters of the future. They live in the here-and-now. Unlike most middle-class individuals, for whom the choice is between short-term gratification and long-term gratification, for them the choice is between short-term gratification and *no* gratification. Typically disenfranchised, the people who most often commit violent crimes don't look at costs and benefits through middle-class lenses.

In the words of Lynn Curtis, president of the Eisenhower Foundation, "To a young man who has a substandard education, few legal-market heroes, and an address in a public housing project with an 80 percent unemployment rate, it is often 'rational' —

that is, consistent with his values and experiences — to choose one or more of the illegal options. Unless advocates of deterrence take greater care to understand how their values and experiences differ from those of inner-city residents, policies against minority crime will continue to be misdirected."

MEASURES THAT BACKFIRE

One of the chief flaws of this strategy, say critics, is that it prescribes tough measures whose consequences are strikingly at odds with their intentions. As an example of get-tough measures that backfire, critics point to mandatory sentencing. Mandatory minimum sentences were intended to be harsh but fair. But the effect of defining specific sentences for certain crimes, say critics, is far different from what is intended. As a result of mandatory minimums, both the courts and the prisons are clogged. Because state prisons are filled with drug addicts and low-level dealers, there is little room for individuals convicted of more serious crimes.

In the words of Robert Gangi, executive director of the Correctional Association of New York, laws that require prison sentences for those convicted of second felony charges fill prisons with the wrong people. As Gangi says, "These laws cause the needless incarceration of people who could be handled more cheaply and effectively through other means."

Since prisons are filled with offenders who pose no particular danger to the public, judges are forced to shave sentences for all criminals to make room. In Florida, critics note that as a result of mandatory minimums enacted in 1987 for drug law violations, prison crowding has become far worse. And it has led to the early release of dangerous felons. Mandatory sentencing has led to a situation in which those who committed violent crimes — about a third of the convicts in state prisons — are recycled more quickly back to the streets.

In much the same way, say critics, long prison terms have a perverse effect. Rather than protecting the public, long prison terms make offenders even more dangerous when they are released. What proponents of longer sentences do not acknowledge, say

critics, is that most convicts eventually get out. At that point, many ex-convicts are more prone to violence than before, and they are very likely to commit another offense.

An April 1989 report from the Justice Department on recidivism — the likelihood of committing a subsequent crime — suggests that longer sentences do little to deter offenders from subsequent crimes. Within three years of their release from state prison, as the report shows, 62 percent of prisoners are arrested again on felony charges, or for a serious misdemeanor. In other words, in more than half the cases in which offenders serve prison sentences, the prison experience fails both as rehabilitation and as a deterrent to subsequent crime.

The report also shows that for those who spent five years in prison, the recidivism rate is roughly the same as for offenders who spent just six months in prison. Critics conclude that our inclination to impose longer sentences as a way of getting tougher on criminals does little to make us safer or to convince most criminals to "go straight."

Indeed, say critics, prison life encourages anti-social tendencies. Psychologist Stanton Samenow, author of a study entitled *Inside the Criminal Mind*, notes that a person behind bars "has ample time and opportunity to learn how to be a better criminal." Prison, he says, is a demoralizing experience that often creates even more anger among convicts. The tension so prevalent in crowded institutions does little to dissuade inmates from violent habits.

During an era of get-tough policies, prisons have become not only more crowded but also harsher places. Since rehabilitation fell into disfavor in the 1970s, the mandate of most prisons has been punishment, plain and simple. In many so-called "correctional institutions," prison-based programs such as remedial education classes, vocational training, mental health services, and substance-abuse counseling have been curtailed. Currently, less than half of all prisoners with a history of drug abuse are enrolled in drug treatment programs. As prisons have become more over-

DANIEL PELAVIN

crowded, less attention is paid to such programs. As a result, inmates in most prisons have fewer opportunities to deal with their personal problems or to gain marketable skills.

What we need to recognize, says Georgetown University sociologist William Chambliss, is that "drug clinics do more to rehabilitate drug addicts than prison; that family counseling reduces family violence more effectively than police; and education, more than any other factor, reduces a propensity to crime."

But our approach to corrections, say critics, is to lock up offenders, to disregard the reasons for their criminal behavior, and to disclaim any responsibility for what might be done to help them straighten out. In the stark words of Norman Carlson, head of the Federal Bureau of Prisons, "Jails are tanks, warehouses. Anyone not a criminal when he goes in will be one when he comes out."

To critics of get-tough policies, it is not surprising that higher incarceration rates over the past decade have been accompanied by higher crime rates. Many inmates complete their prison terms only to commit other serious crimes and return to custody again. "If they don't get any better prepared to face life," says James Waite, an official in Oklahoma's penal system, "then we've just warehoused them for a time. At a cost of about $15,000 per year per inmate, it would be cheaper to send them to college than to keep them in here."

Critics of the get-tough strategy are quick to point out that they recognize the need for prison sentences for dangerous offenders. "None of this argues," says criminologist Elliott Currie, "that we should close all the prisons, nor does it deny that there is a substantial number of people who need to be locked up, some for a very long time. But recognizing that, and coming to terms with the need for prisons, is not the same as believing that building more of them will markedly reduce crime."

Critics conclude that while a policy of more prosecutions, more prisons, and endless sentences may appeal to Americans who are worried about their safety, it does little to deter violent crime. If our goal is to reduce the rate at which serious crime is committed and to make the best use of public funds, a fundamental reappraisal of our approach to criminal justice is needed.

In the words of Ira Glasser, executive director of the American Civil Liberties Union, "Tough talk about violent street crime is popular today. But it deflects attention and resources from real efforts to confront the crime problem. Law enforcement must be as effective as possible. We want to be protected. We want to be able to walk the streets in safety. We want people who commit crimes to be caught, subjected to fair procedures, and punished. But law enforcement by itself cannot control the degradation that's out there in the streets." ■

CHOICE #2
PREVENTIVE STRATEGY:
ATTACKING CRIME AT ITS ROOTS

A second perspective begins with a different view of what the criminal justice system can be expected to accomplish and how to get at the root of the problem. "Street crime cannot be 'solved' by the police, the courts, or prisons," writes Judge David Bazelon of the D.C. Court of Appeals. "Those institutions act as mere janitors, tidying up the wreckage that happens to end up in a courtroom. They cannot begin to address the causes of crime.

"Crime," says Bazelon, "is a human problem indisputably connected with savage social and economic deprivation. The real roots of crime are associated with a constellation of suffering so hideous that, as a society, we cannot bear to look it in the face. So we hand our casualties over to a system that keeps them from sight. If we manage through our exertions to keep up with the criminals, to match their frenzy with our own, we pretend to have solved the crime problem. But to portray such efforts as an 'answer to crime' is a dangerous delusion."

Whereas advocates of our first choice attribute high crime rates to the fact that it is easy to get away with serious acts of violence, advocates of this second perspective insist that crime is a social problem in the deepest sense of the term. In many instances, people resort to crime because of harsh inequalities or their inability to find decent jobs.

Just as we have permitted a bad situation to get worse with regard to the social conditions that provide a breeding ground for crime, say advocates of this approach, the corrections system has done little to help convicts deal with the factors — such as drug addiction or the absence of skills needed in the labor market — that led them to commit criminal acts in the first place. Once individuals enter the criminal justice system, the correc-

"To deal with crime, we must recognize its social roots. The harshness of American society provides a breeding ground for crime, and the corrections system does little to get offenders back on the right path. What is needed is a broad effort to prevent crime."

tional system does little to help them escape a depressingly predictable cycle of crime, imprisonment, release, and the commission of subsequent crimes.

While advocates of this view acknowledge the necessity of protecting the public against dangerous criminals, they favor a fundamentally different approach to sentencing and a radically different crime-prevention strategy. Rather than following the principle of defining punishment to fit the crime, sentencing should be tailored to increase the likelihood that individuals will emerge from the corrections system capable of leading productive, law-abiding lives.

With regard to public efforts to reduce crime, writes Elliott Currie, "while some expenditures must go to improve the capacities of the police and the justice system, more — much more — must go to truly preventive efforts. Those efforts must centrally involve the development of ways to enable the urban young to participate more fully in the social and economic life of the nation."

We can choose, in other words, to mop harder to try to make a difference in the level of the flooding — the get-tough approach to criminal violence. Or we can do something about the open faucet by addressing the social causes of crime.

SINK-OR-SWIM SOCIETY

An accurate diagnosis of America's crime problem, from this perspective, begins with the recognition that the United States is a peculiarly harsh society. As criminologist David Bruck puts it, "If you're going to create a sink-or-swim society, you have to expect people to thrash before they go down." Violent crime represents the thrashing of individuals who see no chance they can make it in a society that offers little encouragement or assistance.

If we want to understand why more violent crime takes place in the United States than in other nations, say advocates of this choice, we have to look beyond the criminal justice system to those features of American society that are different from other industrial nations. From this perspective, many factors in American life — such as a tradition favoring a citizen's right to bear arms — contribute to this nation's predilection for violent crime. But more than anything else, violent crime is a consequence of adverse social and economic conditions. The extreme poverty in which many Americans live, a lack of adequate jobs for family heads, and insufficient public assistance for families under stress all contribute to the high level of criminal violence.

"If we wanted to construct a model of a particularly crime-prone society," writes Elliott Currie, "it would contain these elements: It would separate large numbers of people from the kind of work that integrates them securely into community life. It would promote economic policies that sharply increase inequality. It would shift vast amounts of capital and technology around rapidly without regard for its impact on communities, causing massive movements of population away from family, neighborhood, and community supports in search of livelihood. It would resolutely avoid providing new forms of support and care for those uprooted (in the name of preserving incentives to work and paring government spending). It would promote an ethos of intense competition and a level of material consumption which many citizens cannot lawfully sustain."

No one believes that poverty, the lack of supportive family and community, or the absence of good jobs inevitably leads to crime. But such demeaning circumstances provide a breeding ground for crime. People are far more likely to resort to crime when they lack certain things, such as self-esteem and the promise of advancement through honest work. A society in which many people are deprived of such essentials will, of course, be unusually prone to crime.

The best way to gain an understanding of the source of the problem is to look at the individuals who are the

U.S. CITYSCAPE:

"If you're going to create a sink-or-swim society, you have to expect people to thrash before they go down."

— David Bruck

most frequent perpetrators, and to notice that they frequently come from the bottom of the socioeconomic ladder. "It should not surprise us," as Robert Gangi and Jim Murphy write in a 1990 report by the Correctional Association of New York called *The Imprisoned Generation*, "that the majority of street crimes — the crimes the public fears most — are committed by young men who are out of work and out of school. With no discernible role in mainstream society, many of these young men see no other options for themselves and have been trained to do little else. Prisons are the last stop along a continuum of injustice for these youths that literally starts before birth: no prenatal care, poor health care, substandard housing, dirty streets, failing schools, drugs, joblessness, discriminatory deployment of police. . . . Prisons are the dumping grounds."

Any long-term solution to America's crime problem, from this perspective, must recognize the essence of the problem. The lack of legitimate opportunities — not "sick" personalities, a

genetic predisposition to crime, or the absence of effective deterrents — leads many individuals into lives of crime. Once we recognize that fact, it is obvious that the solution to America's crime problem must emphasize expanded opportunities for advancement.

TROUBLING TRENDS

It is particularly troubling, say advocates of this view, that basic social and economic trends are moving in the wrong direction. Take the phenomenon of growing economic inequality. The United States already has the widest gap between rich and poor of any industrial nation and that gap is growing wider. Americans who have the misfortune of being at the bottom of the income ladder live under greater hardship than their counterparts in other industrial societies.

In various ways, inequality breeds violent crime. It causes bitterness and resentment, and a sense of exclusion on the part of individuals who are unable to participate on an equal basis.

Inequality lowers self-esteem and erodes or destroys the motivation to improve one's situation. Economic deprivation undermines stable families. It is one of the stresses that contributes to domestic violence. And it often leads to alcoholism and drug abuse.

In good economic times and bad ones, but especially when economic growth is sluggish, an increasingly large fraction of the U.S. population faces a bleak job market. Over the past few decades, while white-collar jobs requiring higher education have expanded, manufacturing jobs have disappeared. In every region of the country, more young men are unemployed as a result. The situation of black teenagers — whose unemployment rate in recent years has been double the rate for whites — is worse than ever.

The important thing to note, say advocates of this approach to the crime problem, is that countries with lower levels of violent crime have more humane and effective employment policies. Most industrial nations

23

commit substantial public resources to job training and retraining and have formulated policies to ensure high levels of employment. In the United States, however, such measures have generally been neglected. A high crime rate is part of the price we pay for that neglect.

What must be recognized, writes Elliott Currie, is that "a substantial proportion of disadvantaged young people are offered little more than a choice between inadequate, dead-end work on the one hand and dangerous but lucrative illicit work on the other. Whatever other measures we adopt in the fight against crime, we cannot be wholly successful so long as there are diminishing opportunities for legitimate and rewarding work in the inner cities."

Just as American society in general provides a harsh, crime-prone setting, advocates of this approach point out that the corrections system does little to get offenders back on the right path. In many instances, prison systems offer little or none of the training, education, and support services that can help prepare inmates to lead constructive lives when they are released.

Rather than doing much to address the causes of violent crime, public policy has been, for the most part, reactive. "We wait," says Currie, "for adverse trends to wreak their damage on families and communities. And then we intervene, too little and too late, to deal with the consequences."

Since neither the federal government nor the states have made a serious effort to address the root of corrosive social ills, advocates of this view say that it is no wonder America's anti-crime policy has not worked. In the 1960s, advocates of dealing with the roots of crime insisted that only a "compassionate, massive, and sustained" effort — in the words of the 1968 Kerner Report from the National Advisory Commission on Civil Disor-

der — could keep crime from getting worse. Over the past few decades, the problem has indeed gotten worse.

But there is still only tepid support for the kinds of efforts required to come to grips with crime's causes — such as closing the gap between the haves and have-nots, and providing comprehensive assistance to the underclass, which consists disproportionately of racial minorities. In the words of political scientist Andrew Hacker, author of a recent book *Two Nations: Black and White: Separate, Hostile, and Unequal*, with regard to "sacrifices on behalf of the nation's black minority," he says, "about the only funding the public approves is for more police and prisons."

Because increasingly large amounts are devoted to expanding the corrections system, fewer resources are available to deal with the social roots of the problem. This applies particu-

PAUL CONKLIN

The prison system: reacting to the symptoms of crime, not its roots.

larly to the situation of young black men. "Much of the $7 billion that's spent annually to keep black males incarcerated," writes columnist Calvin Rolark, "could be better used to fund programs to prevent black males from becoming statistics of the criminal justice system."

WHAT SHOULD BE DONE

From this perspective, much of what needs to be done to reduce America's crime problem over the long run falls outside the boundaries of the criminal justice system. A preventive strategy involves halting and reversing several basic trends. As a first step, the growing gap in American society between haves and have-nots must be halted. Among other initiatives, this approach requires a comprehensive employment policy that goes beyond modest current efforts to provide job training. To succeed, such initiatives require the combined resources of government and the private sector in job-creation efforts, to provide accessible and practical retraining for individuals displaced by technological change.

In addition, say advocates of this choice, a major commitment should be made to intensive early education programs for disadvantaged children to break the cycle of poverty. Such efforts, says Elliott Currie, "are preventive — they aim to forestall crime and delinquency before they happen. A much greater emphasis on prevention must be at the heart of any workable strategy against crime."

Similarly, whenever possible, police should take a proactive rather than a reactive approach to crime. Police departments in New York, St. Louis, and other cities, are now experimenting with community-oriented policing as a way of addressing neighborhood problems before they lead to violence. In recent years, police have devoted

"The corrections system must take seriously the task of preparing offenders for rejoining society and playing a productive role in it."

Alternatives to incarceration: A "shock jail" program in Summit, New York

most of their time and energy to responding to repeated service calls — thus becoming, in a frequently heard phrase among enforcement officials, "prisoners of 911." Community-oriented or problem-solving policing requires a significant redefinition of the officer's role. This new role attaches real importance to what police can do to note patterns of crime in a particular neighborhood, and identify and implement solutions to prevent crime. In New Haven, Connecticut, for example, the police department no longer engages in mass drug arrests. Instead, officers go door-to-door in particularly crime-prone neighborhoods, encouraging drug abusers to enter city-sponsored treatment programs.

Concerned on the one hand with preventing crime, this approach to America's crime problem also favors a profoundly different way of dealing with individuals who have broken the law. The objective is to keep criminals from becoming repeat offenders by doing everything possible to reintegrate offenders into the community.

As a priority concern, say advocates of this choice, a harsh and alienating corrections system must be reformed. A more humane system must be created that takes seriously the task of preparing offenders for rejoining society and playing a productive role in it. This means offering programs that take rehabilitation seriously. Some incorrigible criminals are beyond hope. But for most offenders, rehabilitation is a realistic and achievable goal. Criminologist John DiIulio of Princeton University refers to "hundreds of empirical studies" which demonstrate that offenders who take part in carefully designed rehabilitation programs are less likely to commit other crimes.

Except in cases where violent offenders pose a direct threat to the community, the goal of sentencing — in the words of New York federal Judge Jack Weinstein — should be to help offenders get back on their feet, not to knock them to the ground. "Very often the person has a job and a family," says Weinstein. "What you want to do is work with the healthy part, so that the person isn't utterly destroyed."

PRISON CURRICULUM

In particular, this approach emphasizes two initiatives. The first is to reform the corrections system so that it takes seriously the objective of reintegrating offenders into the community. The second is to expand sentencing options to provide alternatives to incarceration.

It is a serious mistake, say proponents of this choice, to run jails and prisons as human warehouses. Jails and prisons should take corrections seriously, and devote more time and money to teaching useful skills and dealing with inmates' problems.

As prisons have become increasingly overcrowded, programs designed to teach work habits and job skills have, in many cases, been cut back. Rooms formerly used as libraries or counseling centers are now filled with bunk beds. Money formerly budgeted for education programs and counseling is used for brick and mortar needed to construct additional cells.

Recently, several states have revived in-prison activities with a correctional emphasis. Corrections facilities in several states now seek arrangements with private employers to contract for inmate labor. In California, voters recently approved a measure permitting private employers to hire inmates to perform various jobs in the prison for at least minimum wages. In a juvenile facility in the Los Angeles area, for instance, 72 young offenders answer calls for TWA's Los Angeles reservations center. Twenty percent of their earnings, which average more than $5 per hour, are paid to the state to cover their room and board at the corrections facility. Another 15 percent is paid into a victim restitution fund.

To advocates of such programs, the point is to offer prisoners work training, to help them gain a better sense of the rhythms and requirements of a regular job. "We want them to hear, see, and smell what private-industry jobs are like," says John Conroy, an officer in the New York State prison system, where inmate industries turn out products ranging from soap to embroidered emblems.

Similarly, say advocates of this approach, prison-based literacy and job-skill programs are a good investment. In Illinois, a new law permits state prisons to require literacy classes for inmates who test at or below the sixth grade reading level.

To help inmates deal with drug and alcohol problems, advocates of this choice also favor expanded counseling and treatment facilities and new inducements for inmates to use such services. Alabama's state prisons are the site of a federally funded drug treatment center which offers intensive treatment programs and counseling. "We don't ask for volunteers," says Dr. Merle Friesen, who directs the facility, "we prescribe it." Initial data from the program suggests that, compared to drug-addicted prisoners who do not go through such treatment, inmates who complete drug treatment are less likely to become repeat offenders.

As part of the anti-crime package he proposes, Congressman Charles E. Schumer of New York City favors mandatory drug treatment for all prisoners with addiction problems in federal facilities. At $3,000 a year per prisoner, drug treatment for all federal prisoners would cost an estimated $120 million annually. Schumer, who cites studies of the effectiveness of such programs, argues that over the long run this is one of the best investments in crime prevention.

From this perspective, prison facilities across the country should provide correctional programs and encourage or require inmates to take advantage of them. Such programs are not mere frills or means of passing time and keeping order in corrections facilities. Helping inmates deal with the source of their problems and learn the skills they will need when released

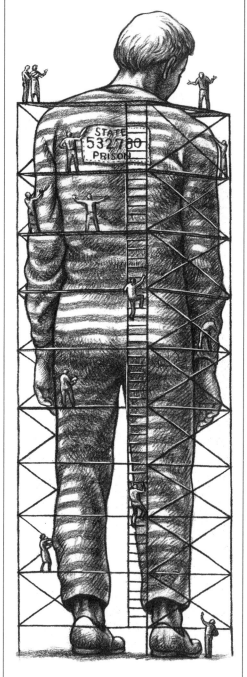

DAVID GOTHARD

"The hope," says Joan Petersilia, "is that these people will become functioning members of the community."

must be an important part of the task of correctional institutions.

SENTENCING ALTERNATIVES

Another change that should be made in the corrections system, say advocates of this choice, is to provide alternatives to incarceration that help offenders become functioning members of the community. While prison is often necessary for violent offenders, it should be only one item on a menu of sentencing alternatives.

As things stand, when judges hand down a sentence in a case involving a moderately serious crime such as burglary or embezzlement, they often face a forced choice between an excessive response and an insufficient one. Offenders are either locked up — some of them for a long time — or they are placed on probation, where they may have no more than perfunctory contact with overloaded probation officers. Defense lawyers aim either to get their clients acquitted or to work out a plea bargain that minimizes prison time, but often does little or nothing to help rehabilitate the offender.

Recognizing the importance of dealing with the underlying causes of criminal behavior, advocates of this choice point out that many offenders would be better served by such sentences as required participation in a drug-treatment program, community service work, or placement in a halfway house that allows them to maintain contact with their families.

The point of alternative sentencing arrangements — which range from community service programs to restitution to victims of crime — is to free up expensive prison space for the most dangerous criminals by devising creative alternatives for other offenders. These alternatives should be tailored to individual criminals to increase the likelihood that they will emerge from the corrections system capable of leading productive, law-abiding lives.

> "Of course we're going to have cases that require severe punishment. But in many cases prison terms may have less impact than alternative, less expensive customized arrangements."
>
> — Steven Goldsmith

In the words of Steven Goldsmith, prosecutor in Marion County, Indiana, "Of course we're going to have Central Park jogger cases that require severe punishment. But in many cases prison terms may have less impact on crime over time than alternative, less expensive customized arrangements."

Advocates point to studies that show the good effects of a variety of alternatives that lie between probation and incarceration, including family counseling and intensive residential care. Some studies suggest that even hard-core violent juvenile offenders are more likely to be dissuaded from future offenses by community-based intensive programs than by prison terms.

Advocates of this choice regard intensive probation as a particularly promising alternative. Under intensive probation supervision programs, participants are typically required to work in gainful employment, to pay restitution to their victims, and — when it is needed — to undergo substance abuse counseling. In contrast to normal probation, in which an officer's caseload might include 150 offenders, under intensive probation an officer supervises no more than about 25 people, seeing each of them as often as 5 times a week. To make sure offenders comply with restrictions imposed by probation, in some cases small radio transmitters are attached to their ankles with tamperproof straps. Participants are expected to comply not only with curfew rules and other expectations about their behavior and whereabouts but also to abstain from alcohol and drug use during the probationary period, and maintain regular work habits. If offenders violate the terms of the program, they are immediately taken to prison.

As a New Jersey official describes that state's Intensive Supervision Program, it is "built around the adage 'firm but fair.' It was meant to be a no-excuses program with a human face. And that's pretty much how it's been run."

Such programs are not cheap. New Jersey's program, for example, costs $6,700 per year per offender to administer. But that's a lot less expensive than what it costs — an estimated $25,000 per offender per year — to keep an inmate in the state's prisons. So far, recidivism rates for graduates of such programs are running at lower rates than among ex-convicts released from prison. Joan Petersilia, a Rand Corporation researcher, says the recidivism rate among those who have experienced intensive probation is impressively low, "usually less than 20 percent."

Advocates of this choice do not necessarily favor all forms of alternative sentencing. They have mixed feelings about the paramilitary training provided in "boot camps." In more than a dozen states, first offenders are sentenced to three to six months in military-style basic training designed to teach discipline and responsible behavior. In Georgia's "shock incarceration" units, for instance, felons spend three months in a program that requires physically demanding military-style calisthenics and hard labor on public-works projects.

Advocates of this perspective concede that the discipline imposed in "boot camps" may be useful. But they doubt that such camps provide what offenders need to successfully return to the community after they have done their time. In the words of Joseph Ingle of the Southern Coalition on Jails and Prisons, "You can't send poor people back to their neighborhoods unable to read and write and expect them to succeed because they have done push-ups."

Successful, well-designed alternatives to incarceration, say advocates of this view, must deal with the roots of crime. "That's the real glimmer of hope," says Joan Petersilia, "that in the long run these people will become functioning members of the community."

No matter how promising alternative sentencing is, say advocates, this strategy won't do much to keep crime rates down until it is applied more widely. The best estimate is that only about 100 such programs are now in place nationwide, involving some 15,000 offenders. Though not yet widely applied, alternative sentencing arrangements are not pie-in-the-sky experiments, say their advocates.

By dealing with the underlying causes, they are consistent with what most Americans regard as the main goal of the criminal justice system — preventing crime. "Hundreds of studies indicate that offenders who participate in alternative sentencing programs are less likely to commit new crimes than comparable offenders who did not participate in them," says John DiIulio, Jr. "This new evidence should cause us to reassess the dismal view of rehabilitation that has prevailed in recent decades."

Advocates point out that programs such as these help to reduce crime rates in a way that is consistent with the values of most Americans. Rather than separating offenders from the community, such programs help to reintegrate them.

Proponents of this approach to crime prevention acknowledge that its results will not be immediately apparent and that it will not be cheap. "Serious preventive programs cost money," says Elliott Currie. "But the question is not whether the money will be spent but how it will be spent. The money can be spent preventively, as a wise investment, or it can be spent reactively and wastefully for increased police and prison cells."

WHAT CRITICS SAY

Those who disagree with this approach to America's crime problem tend to object for the following reasons:

- This strategy, say critics, is naive and unrealistic about the prospect of rehabilitating most individuals who commit serious crimes.
- This approach lets convicted criminals off too easy. Alternative sentences do not adequately convey society's conviction that individuals are responsible for their behavior, and deserve to be punished when they commit crimes.
- By resorting to community-based sentencing for many convicted criminals, this approach releases potentially dangerous criminals back into the community.
- Attempting to prevent crime by engaging in ambitious social engineering will be enormously expensive, and it is not at all certain that such efforts will succeed in reducing the crime rate.
- The real roots of crime are in family life, and there is little public programs can do to intervene at that level.

Most critics of the prevention and rehabilitation approach agree that various anti-crime efforts are worth pursuing. In Memphis, for example, a group called "100 Black Men" is engaged in a mentoring program to provide positive role models to young boys. In Texas, an innovative group therapy program offered at the Giddings State Home and School aims to keep teenaged offenders from becoming repeat offenders by instilling a sense of remorse.

However laudable such efforts are, critics caution that it is unrealistic to expect that much progress can be made through efforts to prevent crime and rehabilitate offenders. It is no doubt true that, with some offenders, when you treat their drug problem you address the underlying cause of criminal behavior. But for many others, say critics, the causes of criminal behavior run much deeper and are not susceptible to change. In the case of hardened criminals, it is unlikely that even the most enlightened prison system could succeed in the task of rehabilitation.

It may be possible, critics concede, to employ alternative sentences for those who commit mild offenses, such as carrying small amounts of drugs. In most cases, however, prison is the only punishment that is appropriately severe, and it is the only sentence that protects the public. Unlike intensive probation, prison keeps criminals off the streets and thus protects everyone else from their predatory behavior.

Do sentencing alternatives allow offenders to get off easy?

The last thing we should do in the name of criminal justice, say critics, is release thousands of potentially dangerous criminals back into the community.

In the words of New York State Senator Dale Volker, "We're willing to do some things to reduce the size of the prison population. But I'm not sure that proponents of sentencing alternatives understand the repercussions of their proposals. We have to be careful that we don't allow dangerous criminals to walk into the community on a regular basis."

Predicting how much danger a particular criminal poses to the community is an inexact science. For this reason, permitting offenders to stay in the community — even if they are under intensive supervision — allows some crimes to be committed that could have been prevented by incarceration.

To convey the impression that alternatives to incarceration are appropriately severe, such programs often carry tough-sounding names. In North Carolina, for example, one plan is called a "community penalties program." But, as critics see it, sentencing alternatives such as intensive probation allow offenders to get off easy. For this reason, they fail to deter other would-be criminals. They fail to convey the fundamental importance of law-abiding behavior, and they do not reflect the threat posed by violent crime. "With these types of sentences," says Gennaro Fischetti, a member of the New York Crime Victims Board, "victims feel they have been betrayed by the system."

A serious drawback of this approach, say critics, is that it overlooks the issue of personal responsibility. "We've got to get back to holding people responsible for their actions," says Reuben Greenberg, chief of police in Charleston, South Carolina. "A guy who pulls a gun in a bank is responsible, not his granddaddy's slavemaster, not the landlord who used lead paint, and not his father who left home. Most kids from broken homes don't commit crimes."

"In most cases, say critics, prison is the only punishment that is appropriately severe, and it is the only sentence that protects the public."

Another weakness of this approach, say critics, is that the social engineering it prescribes would require a massive, long-term effort — with no certainty that crime rates would decrease as a consequence. The likelihood is that, even if job-training programs resulted in a 25 percent reduction in unemployment rates, they would not appreciably affect the underclass, which is the core of the nation's violent crime problem.

As James Q. Wilson comments, little evidence supports the assertion that providing jobs to would-be criminals or to convicted offenders reduces the likelihood that they will commit subsequent crimes. "The hope, widespread in the 1960s, that job-creation and job-training programs would solve many social problems, including crime," Wilson writes, "led to countless efforts to prevent crime by supplying jobs to crime-prone youths. But an evaluation of the results of such programs among poor blacks in Cincinnati and Detroit found no evidence that participation in the Youth Corps had *any* effect on the proportion of enrollees who came into contact with the police. Essentially the same gloomy conclusion was reached by the authors of a survey of a large number of delinquency-prevention programs."

To critics, this search for the roots of crime amounts to "sociologizing" rather than responding to a serious and immediate problem. In a speech that opened the Bush administration's March 1991 anti-crime summit meeting, Attorney General Dick Thornburgh voiced his disdain for such approaches: "We are not here to search for the roots of crime," he said, "or to discuss sociological theory. The carnage in our streets must be halted now."

The purpose of discussing violent crime is to decide what public measures can be taken and, in particular, what government can do about it. A fundamental weakness with this diagnosis of the crime problem, say critics, is that it points to the family roots of criminal behavior — roots that government programs cannot directly influence.

In 1981, the report of the Reagan administration's Task Force on Violent Crime noted that the causes of crime are "said to be found in the weakening of familial and communal bonds, the persistence of unacceptable social disadvantages among some segments of society, and the spread of attitudes that favor immediate over deferred gratification." The task force went on

to say that it had not concerned itself with those factors because "we are not convinced that government, by the invention of new programs or the management of existing institutions, can by itself re-create those familial and neighborhood conditions, those social opportunities, and those personal values that in all likelihood are the prerequisites of tranquil communities."

Recent research, say critics, underscores the family roots of criminal behavior. In January 1992, the Justice Department released a report by Allen Beck showing that more than half of the juvenile delinquents imprisoned in state institutions and more than a third of the adult criminals in local jails and state prisons have immediate family members who have been incarcerated. The most serious offenders among the juvenile delinquents studied had the highest percentage of relatives who had been incarcerated, at 52 percent. Commenting on that study, Terrie Moffitt, a professor of psychology at the University of Wisconsin, said that "This study shows that where you really learn delinquency is from your family."

The implication of such studies, say critics of this approach to crime prevention, is that since the roots of crime lie in family life, government can do little about it. "There are," says James Q. Wilson, "certain things we can change in accordance with our intentions and certain ones we cannot. A free society lacks the capacity to alter the root causes of crime."

One thing we *can* do, however, is incarcerate those individuals who violate the laws, commit serious crime, and threaten the basis of civil society. Critics acknowledge that this is not an appealing way of dealing with a serious problem. But it is realistic. For incorrigible criminals, who are the special concern of advocates of our third choice, it may be the only realistic option. ■

CHOICE #3
SELECTIVE INCAPACITATION STRATEGY: TARGETING THE VIOLENT FEW

"A large part of the crime problem is caused by a small number of repeat offenders. The best way to come to grips with violent crime is to focus enforcement efforts on career criminals, and impose harsh sentences to keep them from committing additional crimes."

In one of his comedy routines, Richard Pryor pauses in the middle of a series of jokes and talks pensively about *Stir Crazy*, a film made several years ago in which he and Gene Wilder starred. To prepare for their roles as men unjustly imprisoned, Pryor and Wilder spent time in an Arizona penitentiary. As Pryor recalls, they talked with men who had been behind bars for years, heard their stories, got to know something about them and their families, caught glimpses of their souls. The experience, said Pryor, made a deep impression and it left him with a message for those who have never had the same experience. The message, said Pryor, was "Thank God for the penitentiary!"

As advocates of a third approach to violent crime see it, anyone who looks closely at the individuals who are responsible for most of these crimes is likely to come away from the experience, as Pryor did, with a different view of what should be done.

As he prepared to write *The Hot House,* a book about Leavenworth prison, journalist Peter Earley spent months talking to inmates about the course of events that led to their incarceration, and how they see themselves. In Earley's words, "Statistics cannot convey the horror of these men's pasts. Nearly all have been psychologically analyzed up, down, over, and under, and have participated in some 'revolutionary' new program that the public was assured would rehabilitate them. Yet virtually all the convicts at the Hot House have proven to be resolute, intractable, irredeemable outlaws. Crime is their chosen occupa-

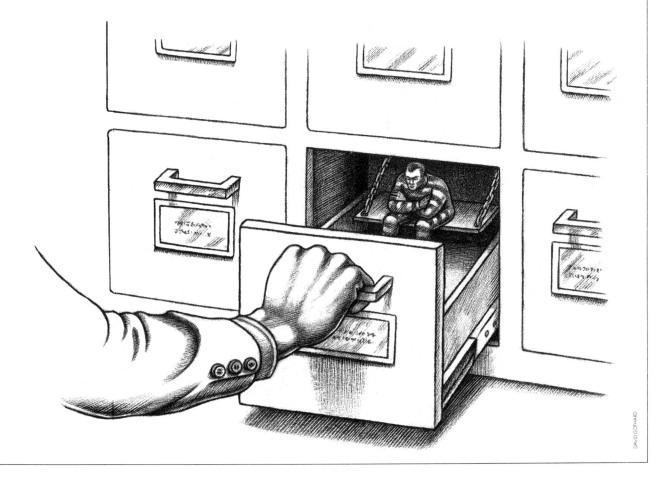

DAVID GOTHARD

tion, violence their tool of choice."

Many of the inmates at Leavenworth, like hardened criminals elsewhere, think of themselves as professionals. Crime is what they "do" — and many have a long list of offenses, ranging from armed robbery and assault to murder. Most began their apprenticeship in crime at an early age, and clearly get a kick out of it. Earley recalls the words of repeat offender William Post: "The truth is, I've always liked living on the edge of madness, being the one out there — the one they are trying to catch — the lone warrior who does his own thing, who answers only to himself."

Earley recalls a note in the file of Carl Bowles, an inmate who has proved to be as uncontrollable inside Leavenworth as he was on the streets, contains this stern message: "This man is ruthless, has no conscience, shows no signs of regret or remorse. He should never be released again in society."

To deal with the problem of violent crime, say advocates of this third choice, we must recognize that the most serious criminals are sociopaths — they are ruthless, they have no conscience, no sense of remorse, and they are irredeemable. A small percentage of these "career criminals" commit a high percentage of all serious crimes.

The most promising way to deal with the crime problem, from this perspective, is to focus the resources of the criminal justice system on these high-rate offenders, while devoting less time (and fewer prison cells) to those who commit less-serious crimes.

This approach to crime differs significantly from the first two positions. It rests on the assertion that the most dangerous criminals are different from other people; they are undeterred by the prospect of being caught and punished, and they cannot be rehabilitated. This strategy suggests different

THE HOT HOUSE LIFE INSIDE LEAVENWORTH PRISON PETE EARLEY Author of FAMILY OF SPIES

USED BY PERMISSION OF BANTAM BOOKS

priorities for law enforcement, and a different principle for sentencing.

From this perspective, both strategies considered so far are hopelessly unrealistic. The prevention and rehabilitation approach we just examined is deeply flawed, in this view, because it naively assumes that individuals who commit serious crimes can, in many cases, be rehabilitated. The get-tough approach is also unrealistic, but for a different reason. Considering how many people are arrested at least once, proponents of this choice conclude that an unselective policy of punishing *all* criminals severely would quickly overwhelm the justice system — and indeed it already has.

In a recent study conducted for California's Bureau of Justice Statistics, criminologist Robert Tillman found that more than a third of all California males between the ages of

18 and 29 are arrested at least once. "Being arrested," Tillman says, "is not an uncommon experience for young adult males in California. If possessing a 'criminal record' is the prime criterion for membership in the 'criminal population,' the size of that population appears to be considerably larger than is generally recognized."

A major implication of such findings, say advocates of this third choice, is that the criminal justice system must become more selective in its enforcement and sentencing procedures. In particular, a distinction needs to be made between those who commit just one or two offenses, and chronic offenders who are responsible for a large fraction of all serious crimes committed in the United States. In the words of Marvin Wolfgang, a criminologist who has conducted landmark studies of the threat posed by repeat offenders, "This is the group that society is afraid of, and rightly so."

What we should do, in brief, is identify the individuals most likely to break the law repeatedly and lock them up for a long period, thus protecting society. Unlike the first two strategies, selective incapacitation, in this view, is both realistic and promising, an idea whose time has come as a solution to an increasingly serious problem.

SUPERFELONS

This choice begins with a distinctive explanation of why people commit serious crimes. Violent crime cannot be explained by a lack of legitimate opportunities. In most instances, people who resort to violent crime are not calculating individuals who figure they can get away with it. The reason crime rates have not been affected by increasingly harsh penalties, advocates of this perspective assert, is that most career criminals are *not* like the rest of us. Something in their psychological or biological

CAPITAL PUNISHMENT:
A NEW HEARING FOR AN OLD QUESTION

When Congress decided to consider a measure to authorize capital punishment for dozens of federal crimes as part of a new anti-crime package, it focused attention on one of the most contentious points in the debate over crime and punishment.

The Bush administration has long favored expanding the death penalty. In the words of former Attorney General Dick Thornburgh, "We need a workable death penalty for terrorist murderers, serial killers, and other heinous criminals."

As a punishment for convicted murderers, a majority of the American public supports the death penalty, too. Support for capital punishment for persons convicted of murder has risen sharply over the past 30 years — from a bare majority of 53 percent in 1960 to a solid majority of 76 percent in 1990, according to polls conducted by the Gallup organization. Judging by a 1990 CBS News/New York Times poll, 60 per-

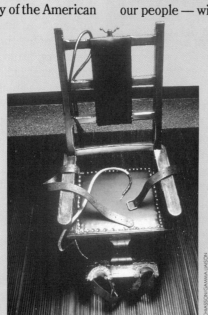

cent of the American public also believes capital punishment is an effective deterrent to murder.

Since 1976, when the Supreme Court ruled in the case of *Gregg* v. *Georgia* that the death penalty is legal and does not necessarily violate the Eighth Amendment's prohibition against cruel and unusual punishment, various states have passed or reenacted capital pun-

ishment laws. While the death penalty is legal today in 37 states and some 2,000 convicted criminals are on "death row," it is not often applied. In none of the past 5 years have more than 25 executions taken place. More than 70 percent of all executions take place in four Southern states — Texas, Louisiana, Georgia, and Florida.

Most advocates of expanding the range of crimes punishable by the death penalty agree with what President Nixon said in the early 1970s in favor of capital punishment: "The only way to attack crime is the way crimes attack our people — without pity."

However, critics strongly oppose the death penalty. It's ineffective, they say. No evidence supports the assertion that it is a uniquely effective deterrent to serious crime. Most murderers, critics say, act impulsively, giving little thought to the consequences of their actions.

More fundamentally, say critics, the death penalty is immoral. In civilized society, we reject the principle of "an eye for an eye." Doing to murderers what they did to their victims is not an act of justice but an act of vengeance, which devalues human life.

"People are understandably frightened and angry about violent crime in this country," says Henry Schwarzschild, head of the ACLU's project on capital punishment. "But the death penalty is not the solution."

makeup causes these individuals to be less influenced by the conventional rewards for good behavior as well as the prospect of being apprehended and punished for breaking the laws.

Some people commit crimes regardless of the risk involved. Indeed, for certain individuals, as the risk increases so does the thrill of committing the crime. Others (particularly those under the influence of drugs or alcohol) seem only dimly aware of the risk they take and the injury inflicted when they commit a crime. In brief, many criminals are deeply disturbed individuals who feel no empathy for their victims and no remorse.

A realistic program of crime control, from this perspective, has to begin with a sober view of human nature that recognizes the existence of evil. As James Q. Wilson puts it in *Thinking About Crime*, an "unflattering view of man" tells us that "wicked people exist" and that "nothing avails us but to set them apart from innocent people." The goal of the criminal justice system, from this perspective, should be to do everything possible to identify incorrigible repeat offenders and throw the book at them.

Pioneering studies conducted by Marvin Wolfgang found that a small number of hard-core offenders are responsible for a substantial fraction of all serious crimes. Wolfgang and his colleagues compiled criminal records for males born in Philadelphia in 1945, and tracked the arrests in which those men were involved until they reached age 30. Wolfgang showed that 35 percent of the group committed just one crime and then were not arrested again. The crux of the crime problem, as Wolfgang found, was a small group of hard-core criminals — about 7 percent of the total — who committed two-thirds of all violent crime, including three-fourths of the rapes and robberies, and virtually all the murders. On average, the individuals in this

> "A distinction needs to be made between criminals who commit just one or two offenses, and dangerous repeat offenders."

hard-core group had been arrested 5 times by age 18. But they continued to commit felonies at a high rate and for each subsequent arrest got away with about a dozen crimes.

The pattern identified by Wolfgang suggests that many violent crimes are committed by a small group of hard-core offenders, those who are accurately described as chronic criminals. Two of the Leavenworth inmates interviewed by Pete Earley are typical. Inmate William Post, the "lone warrior who does his own thing and answers only to himself" has a criminal record dating back to age eight. According to Earley, in addition to arrests for assorted misdemeanors, Post has been arrested for robbery, burglary, assault, and car theft. As for Carl Bowles, he got into trouble with the law at age 8 and was first taken into custody at age 12. As indicated by the documents contained in two thick file folders that describe his arrest record, Bowles is a cop-killer and was found guilty of a triple murder.

Since serious crime is concentrated among repeat offenders, the most effective enforcement strategy is to devote more resources to identify high-rate offenders and put them behind bars for a long time. Researchers at the Rand Corporation who have conducted influential studies in this area refer to this as a strategy of selective incapacitation.

This approach proposes even tougher punishments for repeat offenders, to prevent them from committing further crimes. At the same time, criminals who are not serious or repeat offenders should have their sentences shortened.

The potential benefits of this approach are clear. If hard-core criminals can be identified early in their careers and put behind bars until they are past the most crime-prone years (criminal activity generally declines significantly

LYNN JOHNSON/BLACK STAR

"An unflattering view of man," says James Q. Wilson, tells us that "wicked people exist."

after the age of 30), we should be able to reduce the overall crime rate significantly without spending much more for prisons.

According to Wolfgang's calculations, roughly 75,000 additional hard-core criminals are added to the population each year. They hit their peak rate of committing offenses early, by the age of 16. Since a large number of crimes are committed by this group of superfelons, even a modest improvement in arresting, convicting, and incarcerating such individuals until they reach age 30 would result in a significant reduction in crime.

HIGH-RATE OFFENDERS

The crucial question is whether accurate predictions can be made of which criminals are likely to become high-rate offenders while they are still young, so that harsh sentences can be imposed to prevent a series of

subsequent crimes.

The problem, as advocates of this approach acknowledge, is that it is difficult to predict accurately who the high-rate offenders will be. Knowing the nature of their present offense is not a sufficient clue, because most criminals do not specialize. The individual who snatches a purse today may commit armed robbery tomorrow. So the crime for which an individual is arrested is unlikely to be the same as his or her last crime, or the next one. Accordingly, if sentencing is based mainly on the gravity of the current offense, a person with a long arrest record who is caught for a minor offense such as shoplifting may get off with a light sentence. By the same token, a first-time offender caught for armed robbery might get a long sentence.

The strategy of selective incapacitation requires the judge to go beyond the current offense and take into account the offender's past history and personal characteristics, and on that basis sort out the high-rate offenders from all the others.

Trying to anticipate the future behavior of offenders is nothing new. At each stage in the criminal justice system, judgments have long been made about which offenders pose a grave threat to public safety. Decisions about sentencing routinely take into account not only the severity of the crime but also the potential danger that the offender poses to society. So the justice system already sentences offenders selectively. The question is whether other means of identifying high-rate criminals can be devised that are more effective than rules of thumb that have long been used by judges in sentencing.

In an influential study conducted at the Rand Corporation, Peter Greenwood and his colleagues defined a list of factors that help to predict which offenders are most likely to become chronic offenders. They concluded that an offender falls into the "chronic" category if he or she matches any four of these seven factors. The items include:

- Conviction prior to age 16
- Commitment to a juvenile detention facility
- Use of heroin or barbiturates during a two-year period before the current arrest
- Use of heroin or barbiturates as a juvenile
- Employed for less than half of the two-year period before arrest
- A prior robbery or burglary conviction
- Spent more than half of the preceding two years in jail

Greenwood tested the profile of chronic criminals against the sentences judges gave to 781 convicted robbers and burglars in California. In a high percentage of the cases, the profile accurately predicted who they would be. However, the judges gave long terms to many of the low-rate offenders and short terms to a substantial number of the superfelons.

Largely as a result of Greenwood's profile, selective incapacitation became a popular and influential idea in criminal justice. It differs significantly from traditional incapacitation, according to which the punishment fits the crime, and criminals who commit the same crime can expect generally similar sentences. In contrast, selective incapacitation is prospective. It considers more than the seriousness of the current crime and the offender's past record. Drawing on profiles of high-rate offenders, judges consider such factors as the offender's use of drugs, employment history, and other factors to predict future behavior. To take one example, since drug users are more likely to be repeat offenders, under selective incapacitation they get longer sentences.

To its advocates, the advantages of selective incapacitation are substantial. If, as Philadelphia District Attorney Edward Rendell commented, "We can save the community 100 crimes by putting a repeater away for 5 years," the approach has a lot to recommend it. Peter Greenwood, who conducted Rand's research, estimated in a National Institute of Justice report that a selective incapacitation strategy could reduce California's robbery rate by 20 percent without increasing the total number of robbers incarcerated. In contrast, if the strategy of our first choice were employed, it would require incarcerating as many as four times more offenders to accomplish the same result.

Since this strategy was first put forward in the early 1980s, it has become a major influence in American

BILL SWERSEY/GAMMA LIAISON

law enforcement. In many cities, special police surveillance programs are now in place to identify and incarcerate hard-core career criminals. New York City's Citizens Crime Commission recommended the creation of "career criminal units" in the police

department. In Washington, D.C., a special unit of 60 officers was assigned to a Repeat Offender Project to focus on individuals believed to be committing 5 or more serious crimes per week. Many prosecutors now focus on major offenders to make sure that the resources of the criminal justice system are focused on those individuals who pose the most serious threat.

Advocates point to results in cities that have participated in a Justice Department program focusing on serious habitual offenders. In these cities, police, prosecutors, schools, and welfare and probation workers pooled information and focused on the worst offenders, generally youngsters who had been arrested 3 or more times by age 18. In Oxnard, the only city in California that participated in the program, a concerted effort to put serious habitual offenders behind bars resulted in a 38 percent drop in violent crimes in 1987. Advocates of this approach note that, as a result, Oxnard experienced its lowest crime rate in a decade.

YOUTHFUL OFFENDERS

Since studies of high-rate criminals have shown that repeat offenders typically begin their criminal careers at an early age, this approach has special implications for juvenile justice. For decades, juvenile courts have been guided by the assumption that serving time in prison is not the best way to dissuade youngsters from committing subsequent crimes. Thus, although youths can be tried as adults when they commit felonies such as armed robbery, rape, or attempted murder, sentences are typically milder than they would be if adults committed the same offenses.

In large part because so many serious crimes have been committed in recent years by juveniles, there is growing support for treating them like adults. In Detroit, where 43 youths were killed and 365 wounded in 1990

> "High-rate offenders are a very violent population of nasty, brutal offenders. They begin early in life and should be controlled equally early."
>
> — Marvin Wolfgang

in a severe outbreak of violence, prosecutor Ronald Schigur says that "Kids who are involved in violent crime just don't give a hoot about human life."

One implication of this approach to crime control is that, since repeaters start at an early age, serious juvenile offenders must be treated like adults. High-rate offenders, says Marvin Wolfgang, are "a very violent population of nasty, brutal offenders. They begin early in life and should be controlled equally early."

Chronic criminals often begin by age 13 and hit their peak as robbers and burglars by age 16. Wolfgang concludes that a boy who commits his second serious offense before the age of 15 is likely to commit dozens of offenses by age 30. He advocates that after the third conviction, serious juvenile offenders should be considered adult criminals and sentenced accordingly.

In recent years, many police departments and prosecutors have made a concerted effort to arrest and convict young offenders who fit the violent predator pattern. Departing from a tradition of treating juvenile offenders with kid gloves, in more than 20 states legislators have changed the laws to make it easier to try young criminals as adults.

As advocates of this choice conclude, instead of letting juvenile offenders who pose a serious threat to society off with a slap on the wrist, we should concentrate on incarcerating juvenile offenders who seem likely to become chronics — even if it means giving up on them.

In the future, says Georgette Bennett, a writer and criminal justice consultant, "selective incapacitation may become even more sophisticated and use the results of psychological, metabolic, neurological, and hormonal tests to identify criminals with the most potential for crime."

MARICE COHN BAND/ THE MIAMI HERALD

Carlton Bailey, age 13: charged as an adult with murder for shooting a playmate, because of a criminal record that included auto theft and breaking and entering.

Since this strategy requires locking up repeat offenders for long periods of time, proponents acknowledge that it will not be cheap. But they conclude that this is a price worth paying for increased protection against a group known to be dangerous predators. In the words of Alfred Regnery, former administrator of the Office of Juvenile Justice: "Criminologists have given us important knowledge about who commits crime. If police, prosecutors, and judges put it to work, we could vastly improve the fairness and effectiveness of our criminal justice system, ease prison crowding, and enjoy safer streets and homes."

WHAT CRITICS SAY

Selective incapacitation seems to be a commonsense approach and a course of action that may lower the crime rate. But, like the first two strategies, this choice has its critics. Far from being a good idea whose time has come, many critics regard it as deeply flawed, another fad in criminal justice that is unlikely to deliver what it promises.

This approach to crime is criticized in four respects:

- Not enough is known, say critics, to accurately predict which offenders are most likely to be serious repeat offenders.
- This approach leads to arbitrary and unfairly punitive sentences. Sentences must be based on what offenders are likely to do in the future.
- By focusing on high-rate criminals, this approach justifies stinting on efforts to apprehend and punish other criminals, who may not be as dangerous but still pose a threat to the community and deserve to be punished.
- By concluding that serious crime is often committed by sociopaths, we are likely to disclaim responsibility for social conditions that provide a breeding ground for crime.

Since being lenient is not the cause of the crime problem, say some of these critics, getting tougher with career criminals is no solution. Concentrating the resources of the criminal justice system on hard-core or career criminals won't get us anywhere, says Samuel Walker, "because we are *already* tough on so-called career criminals. They do not slip through unprosecuted and unpunished. Consequently, there is little to be gained by 'getting tough.'"

Critics are especially wary of the assertion that enough is known about patterns of criminal behavior to predict

STATE OF EMERGENCY:
ONE COMMUNITY'S EFFORTS TO CURB GANG VIOLENCE

On July 3, 1991, Enrequeta Duran and her three children were walking home from Las Palmas Park in San Fernando, California, when they were wounded by gunfire in a shootout between two rival gangs. Commenting on the turf war that had been escalating for months between the Shaken Cats Midgets and the San-Fers, San Fernando Police Chief Dominick Rivetti said "This is a classic case of two rival gangs going at it with one another. They miss their target and hit innocent bystanders."

The incident, which was featured on network news, illustrates the public's growing sense of vulnerability to serious crime—and a new willingness to take strict measures to prevent it.

"Gang violence is a very serious problem that affects all of us," says Ramona Ripston, executive director of the Southern California chapter of the American Civil Liberties Union (ACLU). "People want to feel safe as they go about their daily lives, whether it is going to the market for a quart of milk or going to the park to play softball."

The shooting convinced officials in San Fernando that emergency measures were needed to protect the public from further harm. "I will not tolerate the terrorism of the residents in our town," declared San Fernando Mayor Doude Wysbeek. "We will use all our resources to stop gang activity in our parks. We will make sure that our citizens can walk on the streets and go to the park safely."

In September 1991, San Fernando's city council passed an emergency ordinance—which will remain in effect for 10 months—barring members of the Shaken Cats and the SanFers from entering Las Palmas Park. If they are caught in the park, gang members risk a fine of $250. If they refuse to leave, gang members can be arrested.

Encouraged by the fact that Las Palmas Park is once again a safe place for city residents, some people are convinced that gang-restriction ordinances are an effective tool in the battle against crime, justified by the threat posed by violent youth gangs. Soon after San Fernando's emergency ordinance was enacted, Los Angeles City Attorney James K. Hahn proposed a similar but more sweeping ordinance for that city that would bar gang members from all city parks, beaches, and recreation facilities.

Others, however, object to San Fernando's ordinance on the grounds that it tramples on civil liberties. Soon after the ordinance went into effect, the American Civil Liberties Union of Southern California asked a court to strike it down. The restrictive ordinance, as the ACLU sees it, violates constitutional guarantees of freedom of movement, as well as freedom of association and assembly. As the ACLU sees it, by revoking civil liberties in the name of protecting public safety, the ordinance sets a dangerous precedent. Moreover, as spokespersons for the ACLU see it, such ordinances represent nothing more than "Band-Aid" solutions to the problem of gang violence. "Only when society is prepared to address a broad range of difficult dilemmas, ranging from employment to education," in the words of an ACLU report about the ordinance, "will it be possible to come to grips with the underlying causes of gang violence."

which felons will become high-rate offenders. "We were told," says Barry Krisberg, president of the National Council on Crime and Delinquency, "to focus on a few mythical people called 'career criminals.' Police didn't lock them up before because they were out looking for 'casual criminals.' We were told that if we could only lock up enough of these so-called career criminals, we were going to turn the corner on crime. We're still looking for them."

The main reason career criminals are hard to find, say critics, is that "profiles" which were supposed to identify truly dangerous criminals—who would then be given harsh sentences—have turned out to be far less helpful than expected. Even the Rand researchers, who devised the 7-point scale, now acknowledge those weaknesses.

In the words of Andrew von Hirsch, summarizing the work of an expert panel on the topic: "The essential message about selective incapacitation is one of skepticism and caution. Identifying high-risk, serious offenders will be impeded for the foreseeable future by the quality of information available to sentencing courts. The impact of selective incapacitation on crime rates is far below proponents' initial estimates and likely to be quite modest. Far from being the near-panacea some of its advocates have asserted it was, it is a device of limited potential."

No one denies that released inmates, as a group, pose a serious threat to public safety. The problem is that no one knows how to predict which offenders are most likely to become repeat offenders. In the words of Laura Winterfield, a researcher who wrote a report on career criminals for the Vera Institute of Justice: "Given the natural course of events, most juvenile offend-

> "The most glaring flaw in this strategy is that it punishes people not only for what they have done, but for what judges think they *may* do in the future."

ers do not become serious adult of-fenders, and knowledge of the juvenile career does not provide much discrimination between those who become high-rate adults and those who do not. The implications for selective incapacitation are not good."

Few people dispute the assertion that the criminal justice system must deal with a substantial number of people who are evil and incapable of remorse — in Wilson's words, "wicked people." "The problem with this," says Elliott Currie, "is not exactly that it is untrue, but that it's unhelpful. It's pointless to deny that wicked people exist. But a fundamental pessimism about human nature doesn't help us explain why, for example, crime increased so much in the United States in the recent past, or why it's so much higher here than in other comparable societies. Why are some people, in some places, so much more 'prone to evil' than others?"

Finally, say critics, this approach raises fundamental questions about sentencing principles. One test of the criminal justice system is whether it is

effective in apprehending dangerous criminals and protecting the peace. But the system must also be just, and in this crucial respect selective incapacitation fails.

The question is whether it is fair for a low-rate offender who is convicted of a serious crime to receive a shorter sentence (because he is not a threat to become a repeat offender) than someone who is caught for a relatively minor offense but judged to be a probable high-rate offender.

"The decision to designate an individual as a career criminal," writes Susan Estrich, law professor at the University of Southern California, "particularly when that designation brings with it surveillance, denial of bail, refusal to plea bargain, and a longer sentence, is a critically important one. It is problematic, at least, if not intolerable to justify extending an individual's prison term on the grounds that he is very dangerous when there is better than a 50-50 chance that he is not. Both the Constitution and our notion

of justice make clear that it is not enough to be a danger in the future. Criminal punishment must be proportionate to the wrong done."

To critics of selective incapacitation, the most glaring flaw of this strategy is that it punishes people not only for what they have done, but for what they *may* do, what judges think they are *likely* to do in the future. This introduces a dangerously arbitrary judgment into the criminal justice process. What we must acknowledge, say critics, is that neither judges nor psychiatrists can accurately forecast what any individual will do. "The truth of the matter," says Samuel Walker, "is that human behavior is unpredictable. People are exactly as poets and novelists and philosophers have always said they are: quirky, individualistic, and highly idiosyncratic. Their behavior does not conform to scientific predictions." To punish some criminals more harshly than others because of their potential for committing serious crimes violates the principle that the punishment should fit the crime.■

VERDICT ON CRIME CONTROL: YOU BE THE JUDGE

"A new consensus is needed about which strategy is most promising, what costs we are willing to pay, and what trade-offs we are willing to accept. Our response will determine whether American society becomes safer, or even more fearful and crime-ridden."

In March 1991, just a few days after allied forces defeated Iraq in the Gulf War, President Bush spoke to a group of law enforcement officials from across the country at a "crime summit" meeting in Washington. The president referred to news reports that during the three days of the ground offensive, more Americans were killed in violent episodes in several American cities than were killed on the frontline in the Gulf War. "Think of it," said the president. "A brave American soldier may have actually been safer in the midst of the largest armed offensive in history than he would have been on the streets of his own hometown. It is outrageous. It is wrong. And it is going to change."

"That," said the president, "is why you have been invited to this unprecedented 'council of war': to share ideas and successes and to help frame the battle plan for the fight against violent crime in the next decade and beyond."

Whatever their thoughts about how to wage the battle against violent crime, most Americans hardly need to be reminded about the threat of crime and the fear it inspires. Prominently displayed at the Washington headquarters of the Justice Department is a "crime clock" — a measure of how often violent crime occurs in the United States. In the mid-1980s, during a 4-year period when the incidence of violent crime fell by more than 10 percent, that clock showed a hopeful trend. It appeared that the nation had turned the corner on crime. Unfortunately, that trend didn't last. The number of violent crimes committed each year is not only on the rise again, it is higher than ever. By March 1992, the "crime clock" showed that a burglary takes place somewhere in the United States every 10 seconds, a rape

"Your honour, we find the defendant guilty, the court room jammed, the docket overloaded, the calendar crowded, the jails full, the system appalling, but, what can you do?"

every 5 minutes, and a murder is committed every 22 minutes. The figures change slightly from time to time, but one thing remains the same: America's dubious distinction as the most violent of industrial nations.

One can only feel troubled by the implications of that stark fact and by the prospect of living in a nation where serious crime is even more common than it is today. "Barring substantial changes in our current policies," says Elliott Currie, "the situation is likely not only to continue but to worsen — with grim and pervasive effects on the quality of American life. Our response to the problem of serious crime will determine whether America in the twenty-first century is a safer society or a more fearful one."

Unfortunately, many discussions of the crime problem consist of little more than pointing the finger of blame. Some people blame a lax criminal justice system, or procedural rules that give criminals the upper hand over law enforcement officials. Others regard the high crime rates as a sign that American society as a whole — families, schools, and churches — no longer attaches much importance to teaching discipline and self-restraint.

Still others, such as criminologist David Bayley, look at this unsavory seam in American life and conclude that it is the inevitable consequence of values America prizes such as individualism, mobility, suspicion of authority, and a tradition of bearing arms. As Bayley concludes, "The United States may have a high level of criminality because it is inhabited by Americans." In which case, it seems reasonable to conclude, little can be done about it.

Most people, however, are not content to end the discussion on that note or to conclude that a disturbingly high level of crime in American life results from forces that are beyond the reach of public policy. If certain

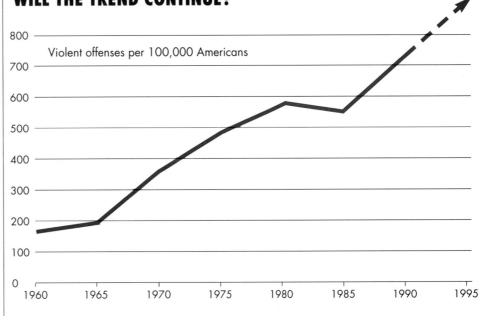

VIOLENT CRIME IN AMERICA: WILL THE TREND CONTINUE?

Violent offenses per 100,000 Americans

Source: U.S. Department of Justice, Federal Bureau of Investigation, Uniform Crime Report

changes are made, most people are convinced that the crime rate could be lowered. The disagreement is over what can and should be done, and what we are prepared to do to achieve that goal.

In recent years, the United States has been pouring a lot of resources into fighting a war on crime. But the results of a tough anti-crime policy have been inconclusive and no one is satisfied. There is general agreement that the crime rate is unacceptably high. Judging by the results of recent surveys, there is also a resounding lack of confidence in the criminal justice system. But there is no consensus about what should be done next or which course of action is most promising. The question is what direction should be taken now in the war on crime.

THREE ALTERNATIVES

Among the three perspectives we have examined, the differences are not superficial or merely tactical. Advocates of each perspective give distinctive answers to fundamental questions about such matters as why people commit crime, what principles should guide sentencing decisions, and whether we should continue to rely heavily on incarceration as the principal sentencing alternative for most offenders.

Each of these strategies involves certain costs and trade-offs. In an important respect, the debate consists of comparing the costs and trade-offs and deciding which we are prepared to live with as the price of achieving safer, less crime-ridden communities.

Getting tougher with *all* criminals to convey the message that society will not tolerate such behavior is a straightforward strategy for reducing violent crime, and one that seems promising to many people. But it would be difficult and costly to bolster enforcement efforts and criminal prosecution to the point where substantially more criminals are arrested and convicted. Stepping up incarceration enough to substantially reduce the crime rate would involve a further dramatic expansion of prison and jail cells, at a time when states are already hard-pressed to pay for the growing cost of the corrections system. If, as proposed by advocates of the first choice, some of the current constraints on the criminal justice system are removed to make it easier to apprehend and convict dangerous criminals, this approach is likely to result in infringements on personal freedoms.

Advocates of our second choice favor a crime-reduction strategy that places far more emphasis on prevention, rehabilitation, and dealing with the social conditions that lead to crime. Putting this approach into practice would be expensive, and in all probability the impact on crime-reduction would not be quickly discernible. The expense of social programs designed to reduce crime by closing the gap between the haves and have-nots and providing new employment opportunities to millions of Americans would be hard for elected officials to justify at a time of record deficits and sharp public resistance to higher taxes. And since advocates of the second choice favor community-based sentencing alternatives for less serious offenders, this choice entails certain risks to public safety as well.

To proponents of selective incapacitation, a more realistic alternative is to concentrate law enforcement resources on a relatively small number of chronic criminals, and to acknowledge that with such incorrigibles there is no alternative but to lock them up for extended prison terms. Since this strategy would put some offenders behind bars for longer terms, it too

would be costly, even though part of the cost might be offset by giving shorter sentences to less serious offenders. Moreover, since this approach favors more severe sentences for juvenile offenders, it amounts to "writing off" some youngsters who under the current system are treated more leniently and given another chance. Since it involves sentencing on the basis of predictions about future criminal activities, this approach would also be unfair in cases where severe sentences are given to individuals who are not chronic offenders.

These three approaches to crime prevention raise practical questions about what can be done to deter crime. They also raise moral questions about what should be done. These questions, in turn, are related to larger disagreements about the kind of society we want for ourselves and our children, and what kinds of trade-offs we are prepared to make — for example, between crime reduction and civil liberties.

WHAT'S MOST PROMISING?

When asked to choose among these alternatives, people commonly respond by saying we should pursue all three — that we should step up enforcement and give harsher sentences, devote special attention to identifying *and* incarcerating high-rate offenders, and make a serious effort to deal with the social conditions that provide a breeding ground for crime.

While some elements of these approaches might be combined, a choice among them is necessary. Choices have to be made about how to put tax dollars to their best use. If our goal is to reduce the crime rate, public resources must be targeted to areas of genuine need. This means trying to achieve a consensus about what kinds

of initiatives are most promising, what costs we are willing to pay, and what trade-offs we are willing to make.

If you ask corrections officials what needs to be done with the criminal justice system, most reply that crowding of correctional institutions is the immediate concern. The main question seems to be where to find the resources to build new or expanded facilities.

But the public needs to consider more fundamental questions: What direction should the criminal justice system take? What strategy is most promising as a way of controlling crime — not just this week and next but over the next decade and into the next century?

As we confront the problem of violent crime and consider the alternatives in responding to it, the question is which direction best reflects the various values we hold — including the value we place on due process, on swift and certain justice, on community safety, on rehabilitating offenders, and on retribution for those who break the laws and shatter the peace.

"Unfortunately," writes Marc Mauer, director of the Sentencing Project, "the decision-making process in criminal justice is particularly prone to the influence of political rhetoric. It is no accident that, for several sessions now, a major crime bill has been adopted by Congress every two years prior to the November election. As the Willie Horton episode showed too well in the last presidential campaign, public policy on issues of crime and justice is far too often driven by the atypical, sensational 'crime of the month,' rather than by a rational examination of the choices."

As Mauer concludes, "We now have the opportunity and the obligation to review our options with regard to crime and punishment, and to examine carefully the lessons of the past decade." ■

FOR FURTHER READING

For a critical examination of liberal and conservative crime-control strategies, see Samuel Walker's *Sense and Nonsense About Crime: A Policy Guide* (Pacific Grove, CA: Brooks/Cole Publishing Company, 1989). John Doble's *Crime and Punishment: The Public's View* (New York: The Public Agenda Foundation, 1987), provides a review of public opinion on a wide range of criminal justice issues.

Two recent publications, John J. DiIulio's *No Escape: The Future of American Corrections* (New York: Basic Books, 1991), and Stephen D. Gottfredson and Sean D. McConville's *America's Correctional Crisis* (New York: Greenwood Press, 1987), explore the dilemmas posed by overcrowded prisons.

For a description of trends in violent crime, see two Bureau of Justice Statistics reports: "Violent Crime in the United States," (Washington, D.C.: U.S. Department of Justice, March 1991) and "Crime Victimization 1990," (Washington, D.C.: U.S. Department of Justice, October 1991). Christopher Jencks puts these statistics in perspective in his article, "Is Violent Crime Increasing?" which appeared in the Winter 1991 issue of *The American Prospect*.

In his influential book *Thinking About Crime* (New York: Basic Books, 1983), James Q. Wilson argues that criminal activity is shaped by the rewards it offers and by the penalties imposed by the criminal justice system. In *Crime and Human Nature* (New York: Simon & Schuster, 1985), Wilson and Richard J. Herrnstein examine the causes of crime. In "Public Safety in the Nineties" (Washington, D.C.: U.S. Department of Justice, 1991), a report on the proceedings of

the 1991 "crime summit," former Attorney General Dick Thornburgh and other law enforcement officials discuss strategies for combating violent crime.

In *The Justice Juggernaut* (New Brunswick: Rutgers University Press, 1990), Diana R. Gordon criticizes the "get-tough" approach to criminal justice. Marc Mauer's, *Americans Behind Bars: A Comparison of International Rates of Incarceration* (Washington, D.C.: The Sentencing Project, 1991), examines the consequences of relying so heavily on prison terms as a means of controlling crime.

In *Confronting Crime: An American Challenge* (New York: Pantheon Books, 1985), Elliott Currie examines social and economic developments that have contributed to America's high crime rate, and lays out a socially oriented strategy for preventing it. In *Young Black Men and the Criminal Justice System: A Growing National Problem* (Washington, D.C.: The Sentencing Project, 1990), Marc Mauer describes the plight of young black males and explains why they are so often involved in crime.

For two books that explore alternative sentencing, see Norval Morris and Michael Tonry's *Between Prison and Probation* (New York: Oxford University Press, 1990) and *Punishing Criminals* (New York: The Public Agenda Foundation, 1991), by John Doble, Stephen Immerwahr, and Amy Richardson.

From the perspective of our third choice, see Peter Greenwood and

Allan Abrahamse's influential report, "Selective Incapacitation" (Santa Monica: Rand Corporation, 1982). In *Delinquency in a Birth Cohort* (Chicago: University of Chicago Press, 1972), Marvin E. Wolfgang and colleagues conclude that a high percentage of serious crimes are committed by a small number of repeat offenders.

In "Selective Incapacitation: A Sheep in Wolf's Clothing?" *Judicature* (October/November 1984), Brian Forst argues that crime-fighting efforts should focus on identifying and locking up the violent few. In *Dangerous Offenders: The Elusive Target of Justice* (Cambridge, MA: Harvard University Press, 1984), Mark H. Moore and his colleagues explore policy implications of selective incapacitation.

In "Selective Incapacitation Reexamined," which appeared in *Criminal Justice Ethics*, (Winter/Spring 1988), Andrew von Hirsch argues that selective incapacitation is unjust because of difficulties in predicting high-rate criminals.

For a vivid description of prison life, see Pete Earley's *The Hot House: Life Inside Leavenworth Prison* (New York: Bantam Books, 1992).

ACKNOWLEDGMENTS

A note of thanks to the colleagues and consultants who helped as we prepared this issue book. Once again, David Mathews and Daniel Yankelovich provided guidance and support. Our colleagues John Doble, Jean Johnson, Jon Rye Kinghorn, Robert Kingston, Suzanne Morse, Patrick Scully, and Deborah Wadsworth played a valuable role in refining the framework and clarifying the presentation. Special thanks to reviewers Loren Siegel and Elliott Currie.

NATIONAL ISSUES FORUMS

The National Issues Forums (NIF) program consists of locally initiated Forums and study circles which bring citizens together in communities throughout the nation for nonpartisan discussions about public issues. In these Forums, the traditional town meeting concept is re-created. Each fall and winter, three issues of particular concern are addressed in these groups. The results are then shared with policymakers.

More than 3,000 civic and education organizations — high schools and colleges, libraries, service organizations, religious groups, and other types of groups — convene Forums and study circles in their communities as part of the National Issues Forums. Each participating organization assumes ownership of the program, adapting the NIF approach and materials to its own mission and to the needs of the local community. In this sense, there is no one type of NIF program. There are many varieties, all locally directed and financed.

Here are answers to some of the most frequently asked questions about the National Issues Forums:

WHAT HAPPENS IN FORUMS?

The goal of Forums and study circles is to stimulate and sustain a certain kind of conversation — a genuinely useful conversation that moves beyond the bounds of partisan politics and the airing of grievances to mutually acceptable responses to common problems. Distinctively, Forums invite discussion about each of several choices, along with their cost and the main arguments for and against them. Forum moderators encourage participants to examine their values and preferences — as individuals and as community members — and apply them to specific issues.

CAN I PARTICIPATE IF I'M NOT WELL INFORMED ABOUT THE ISSUE?

To discuss public issues, citizens need to grasp the underlying problem or dilemma, and they should understand certain basic facts and trends. But it isn't necessary to know a great deal about an issue. NIF discussions focus on what public actions should be taken. That's a matter of judgment that requires collective deliberation. The most important thing to ponder and discuss is the kernel of convictions on which each alternative is based. The task of the National Issues Forums is not to help participants acquire a detailed knowledge of the issue but to help people sort out conflicting principles and preferences, to find out where they agree and disagree and work toward common understandings.

ISN'T ONE PERSON'S OPINION AS GOOD AS ANOTHER'S?

Public judgment differs from personal opinion. It arises when people sort out their values and work through hard choices. Public judgment reflects people's views once they have an opportunity to confront an issue seriously, consider the arguments for and against various positions, and come to terms with the consequences of their beliefs.

ARE FORUM PARTICIPANTS EXPECTED TO AGREE UPON A COURSE OF ACTION?

A fundamental challenge in a democratic nation is sustaining a consensus about a broad direction of public action without ignoring or denying the diversity of individual preferences. Forums do not attempt to achieve complete agreement. Rather, their goal is to help people see which interests are shareable and which are not. A Forum moderator once described the common ground in these words: "Here are five statements that were made in our community Forum. Not everyone agreed with all of them. But there is nothing in them that we couldn't live with."

WHAT'S THE POINT OF ONE MORE BULL SESSION?

Making choices is hard work. It requires something more than talking about public issues. "Talking about" is what we do every day. We talk about the weather, or our friends, or the government. But the "choice work" that takes place in Forum discussions involves weighing alternatives and considering the consequences of various courses of action. It means accepting certain choices even if they aren't entirely consistent with what we want, and even if the cost is higher than we imagined. Forum participants learn how to work through issues together. That means using talk to discover, not just to persuade or advocate.

DO THE FORUMS LEAD TO POLITICAL ACTION?

Neither local convenors nor the National Issues Forums as a whole advocate partisan positions or specific solutions. The Forums' purpose is to influence the political process in a more fundamental way. Before elected officials decide upon specific proposals, they need to know what kinds of initiatives the public favors. As President Carter once said, "Government cannot set goals and it cannot define our vision." The purpose of the Forums is to provide an occasion for people to decide what broad direction public action should take.

CRIMINAL VIOLENCE:
WHAT DIRECTION NOW FOR THE WAR ON CRIME?

One of the reasons people participate in the National Issues Forums is that they want leaders to know how they feel about the issues. So that we can present your thoughts and feelings about this issue, we'd like you to fill out this ballot before you attend Forum meetings (or before you read this book if you buy it elsewhere), and a second ballot after the Forum. Before answering any of the questions, make up a three-digit number and fill it in the box below.

The moderator of your local Forum will ask you to hand in this ballot at the end of the session. If you cannot attend the meeting, send the completed ballot to National Issues Forums, 100 Commons Road, Dayton, Ohio 45459-2777.

Fill in your three-digit number here [   ]

1. Which of the following are the most important causes of violent crime:

	Most Important	Somewhat Important	Not At All Important
a. Criminals think they can get away with crime, or at least get off easy if caught.	☐	☐	☐
b. Social and economic problems such as the breakdown of the family, the prevalence of drugs, and joblessness.	☐	☐	☐
c. The criminal justice system is more concerned with legal technicalities (such as how evidence was obtained) than with real justice.	☐	☐	☐
d. The criminal justice system fails to keep chronic criminals who are responsible for a majority of violent crime locked up.	☐	☐	☐

2. Below are different approaches this nation can take in dealing with crime, each one involving trade-offs and sacrifices. Please rank the approaches on a 1 to 3 scale, with 1 being the approach you prefer most and 3 being the approach you favor least:

Deterrence is the basis of any effective crime strategy: we need to make it easier to apprehend, convict, and keep criminals in jail, *even if* this means more restrictions on our civil liberties.   _____

To make real progress with crime we must deal with the root societal problems which cause it: we need programs which deal with the lack of education and jobs, poverty and social inequalities, *even if* these programs will be costly.   _____

We need to focus the resources of the criminal justice system on violent, repeat offenders, *even if* this means devoting fewer resources to less serious criminals.   _____

3. Here are some arguments for and against **Choice #1 — Deterrent Strategy: Getting Tougher on Criminals.** Whether you favor this choice or not, please indicate whether you agree or disagree with the following arguments. (Check one for each argument.)

	Agree	Disagree	Not Sure
a. Mandatory sentencing will improve the public's safety by making sure individuals who commit serious crimes serve time in prison and are removed from contact with the community.	☐	☐	☐
b. Building more prisons and imposing harsher sentences on offenders will not reduce crime — as long as the root causes of crime are unaddressed, new criminals will simply take the place of those in prison.	☐	☐	☐
c. The idea of simply putting all criminal offenders in prison is an appealing but counterproductive solution — many offenders become hardened and more dangerous as a result of being in prison.	☐	☐	☐

4. Here are some arguments for and against **Choice #2 — Preventive Strategy: Attacking Crime at Its Roots.** Whether you favor this choice or not, please indicate whether you agree or disagree with the following arguments. (Check one for each argument.)

	Agree	Disagree	Not Sure
a. In the long run, it will cost less to rehabilitate offenders and make them contributing members of society than to keep them locked up.	☐	☐	☐
b. Rehabilitation programs in prisons will not change the criminal behavior of most serious offenders — they must be isolated from the community.	☐	☐	☐
c. Trying to fight crime with programs aimed at serious social problems such as drugs and the breakdown of the family will cost a lot of money and accomplish very little.	☐	☐	☐

5. Here are some arguments for and against **Choice #3 — Selective Incapacitation Strategy: Targeting the Violent Few.** Whether you favor this choice or not, please indicate whether you agree or disagree with the following arguments. (Check one for each argument.)

	Agree	Disagree	Not Sure
a. A small number of offenders are responsible for a disproportionate amount of violent crime: focusing our limited resources on these criminals is the most realistic hope we have for making our society safer.	☐	☐	☐
b. By concentrating our resources on isolating a group of violent, repeat criminals rather than dealing with the social conditions which create them, we all but guarantee that the crime problem will worsen.	☐	☐	☐
c. Selective incapacitation requires judges to assess a criminal's violent potential — some people might receive arbitrary or unfair sentences.	☐	☐	☐

6. In your community, do you think that violent crime is more of a problem than it was ten years ago, less of a problem than ten years ago, or is it about the same? (Check one.)

- **a.** More ☐
- **b.** Same ☐
- **c.** Less ☐
- **d.** Not Sure ☐

7. In the last year or so, have you or has anyone in your immediate family been the victim of a violent crime? (Check one.)

- **a.** Yes ☐
- **b.** No ☐
- **c.** Not Sure ☐

8. Which of these age groups are you in? (Check one.)

- **a.** Under 18 ☐
- **b.** 18-29 ☐
- **c.** 30-44 ☐
- **d.** 45-64 ☐
- **e.** 65 or over ☐

9. Are you a:

- **a.** Man ☐
- **b.** Woman ☐

10. Do you consider yourself: (Check one.)

- **a.** White ☐
- **b.** Black or Afro-American ☐
- **c.** Hispanic ☐
- **d.** Asian ☐
- **e.** Other (Specify:_____) ☐

11. What is your ZIP CODE? _____

POST-FORUM BALLOT

CRIMINAL VIOLENCE:
WHAT DIRECTION NOW FOR THE WAR ON CRIME?

Now that you've had a chance to read the book or attend a Forum discussion we'd like to know what you think about this issue. Your opinions, along with thousands of others who participated in this year's Forums, will be reflected in a summary report prepared for participants as well as elected officials and policymakers working on this problem. Some of these questions are the same as those you answered earlier. Before answering any of the questions, write your three-digit number in the box below.

Please hand this to the Forum leader at the end of the session, or mail it to National Issues Forums, 100 Commons Road, Dayton, Ohio 45459-2777.

Fill in your three-digit number here ☐

	Most Important	**Somewhat Important**	**Not At All Important**
1. Which of the following are the most important causes of violent crime:			
a. Criminals think they can get away with crime, or at least get off easy if caught.	☐	☐	☐
b. Social and economic problems such as the breakdown of the family, the prevalence of drugs, and joblessness.	☐	☐	☐
c. The criminal justice system is more concerned with legal technicalities (such as how evidence was obtained) than with real justice.	☐	☐	☐
d. The criminal justice system fails to keep chronic criminals who are responsible for a majority of violent crime locked up.	☐	☐	☐

2. Below are different approaches this nation can take in dealing with crime, each one involving trade-offs and sacrifices. Please rank the approaches on a 1 to 3 scale, with 1 being the approach you prefer most and 3 being the approach you favor least:

Deterrence is the basis of any effective crime strategy: we need to make it easier to apprehend, convict, and keep criminals in jail, *even if* this means more restrictions on our civil liberties. _____

To make real progress with crime we must deal with the root societal problems which cause it: we need programs which deal with the lack of education and jobs, poverty and social inequalities, *even if* these programs will be costly. _____

We need to focus the resources of the criminal justice system on violent, repeat offenders, *even if* this means devoting fewer resources to less serious criminals. _____

3. How do you think your **discussion group** ranked the three approaches on a 1 to 3 scale?

Deterrence is the basis of any effective crime strategy: we need to make it easier to apprehend, convict, and keep criminals in jail, *even if* this means more restrictions on our civil liberties. _____

To make real progress with crime we must deal with the root societal problems which cause it: we need programs which deal with the lack of education and jobs, poverty and social inequalities, *even if* these programs will be costly. _____

We need to focus the resources of the criminal justice system on violent, repeat offenders, *even if* this means devoting fewer resources to less serious criminals. _____

4. Here are some arguments for and against **Choice #1 — Deterrent Strategy: Getting Tougher on Criminals.** Whether you favor this choice or not, please indicate whether you agree or disagree with the following arguments. (Check one for each argument.)

	Agree	Disagree	Not Sure
a. Mandatory sentencing will improve the public's safety by making sure individuals who commit serious crimes serve time in prison and are removed from contact with the community.	☐	☐	☐
b. Building more prisons and imposing harsher sentences on offenders will not reduce crime — as long as the root causes of crime are unaddressed, new criminals will simply take the place of those in prison.	☐	☐	☐
c. The idea of simply putting all criminal offenders in prison is an appealing but counterproductive solution — many offenders become hardened and more dangerous as a result of being in prison.	☐	☐	☐

5. Here are some arguments for and against **Choice #2 — Preventive Strategy: Attacking Crime at Its Roots.** Whether you favor this choice or not, please indicate whether you agree or disagree with the following arguments. (Check one for each argument.)

	Agree	Disagree	Not Sure
a. In the long run, it will cost less to rehabilitate offenders and make them contributing members of society than to keep them locked up.	☐	☐	☐
b. Rehabilitation programs in prisons will not change the criminal behavior of most serious offenders — they must be isolated from the community.	☐	☐	☐
c. Trying to fight crime with programs aimed at serious social problems such as drugs and the breakdown of the family will cost a lot of money and accomplish very little.	☐	☐	☐

6. Here are some arguments for and against **Choice #3 — Selective Incapacitation Strategy: Targeting the Violent Few.** Whether you favor this choice or not, please indicate whether you agree or disagree with the following arguments. (Check one for each argument.)

	Agree	Disagree	Not Sure
a. A small number of offenders are responsible for a disproportionate amount of violent crime: focusing our limited resources on these criminals is the most realistic hope we have for making our society safer.	☐	☐	☐
b. By concentrating our resources on isolating a group of violent, repeat criminals rather than dealing with the social conditions which create them, we all but guarantee that the crime problem will worsen.	☐	☐	☐
c. Selective incapacitation requires judges to assess a criminal's violent potential — some people might receive arbitrary or unfair sentences.	☐	☐	☐

7. What is your ZIP CODE? _____